CONTENTS

INTRODUCTION
4

STEP-BY-STEP TECHNIQUES GUIDE
5

APPETISERS
10

MAIN COURSES
20

ACCOMPANIMENTS
36

DESSERTS
44

PRESERVES AND SWEETS
56

BAKING
66

INDEX
80

COOKERY NOTES

- Both metric and imperial measures are given for the recipes. Follow either metric or imperial throughout as they are not interchangeable.
- All spoon measures are level unless otherwise stated. Sets of measuring spoons are available in metric and imperial for accurate measurement of small quantities.
- Ovens should be preheated to the specified temperature. Grills should also be preheated. The cooking times given in the recipes assume that this has been done.

- Where a stage is specified in brackets under freezing instructions, the dish should be frozen at the end of that stage.
- Size 2 eggs should be used except where otherwise specified. Free-range eggs are recommended.
- Use freshly ground black pepper unless otherwise specified.
- Use fresh rather than dried herbs unless dried herbs are suggested in the recipe.

INTRODUCTION

Christmas is our most celebrated holiday – a time when families spend a few days of concentrated eating, drinking and merrymaking together. Of course this can lead to a great deal of stress and anxiety, especially for the hosts, but with careful planning and job-sharing, the preparations can be fun, leaving time to relax and enjoy the festivities!

In this book I've tried to create recipes that depart a little from the traditional, and give old favourites a new slant. Pickled Salmon on Rye, for example, is a wonderfully easy homemade version of Gravad Lax, which not only tastes delicious, but can be made well in advance ready for a starter, or an impromptu drinks party!

The recipes make good use of the seasonal foods readily available at this time of year, with a few exotic additions, such as star fruit and fresh dates, that have started to creep into our supermarkets. I've given alternative suggestions for foods that may not be so readily available, and time-saving options where appropriate. For example, fresh chestnuts taste fantastic – especially when roasted on the fire – but not all of us have real fires now, and shelling chestnuts to make a stuffing or soup is a real bore! Ready-prepared vacuum-packed chestnuts are an excellent, although more expensive, alternative. Start building up a storecupboard of useful ingredients well in advance, when you come across things you might need – this will also help spread the cost.

You will find a range of recipes to suit all purses and occasions, from the homely and comforting Turkey Pot Pie to the extravagant French Roast Pheasant with Grapes and Walnuts. For your festive dinner, choose the traditional Roast Turkey with all the trimmings; or an Old English Roast Rib of Beef served with a deliciously different relish of chestnuts and pickled walnuts; or an elegant Baked Salmon with Saffron Hollandaise, if you prefer. For vegetarians, there is a richly satisfying Vegetable Ragoût with Cheese Polenta Topping.

This is also the season for ridiculously rich and luscious puddings, and there are several here to tempt you. Those who have just had enough might find the refreshing fruit salad with honeyed kumquats more appealing!

Christmas wouldn't be the same without the traditional festive bakes, and these also make pleasing gifts both to give and receive. Throughout the year, collect small empty boxes and pretty bits of ribbon or bows from other presents to use in some way to decorate your gifts. Spray boxes white, gold or silver, if you like. A little glitter used judiciously can have a wonderful magical effect! Line boxes and baskets with shredded tissue. Alternatively, simply wrap items neatly in waxed or greaseproof paper and tie with a simple ribbon. Truffles, Scots Tablet, Shortbread, chutneys and bottled fruits all make good gifts. Quick Curried Nuts and Marinated Olives are ideal presents too, packed in pretty tins or jars with festive ribbon.

Make the advent of Christmas special for the children by making the Gingerbread Nativity with them. The dough is simplicity itself and can be frozen. Once you have assembled the stable, the figures can be made a few at a time, and should be decorated as simply as possible for maximum effect. Make sure decorations are edible unless of course, you make it known that the figures are not to be eaten.

Organisation is the key to an enjoyable holiday – do as much as possible in advance – and delegate! Improvise if more storage space is needed – put cold drinks in a garden shed or greenhouse or even outside on window sills to relieve congestion in the fridge. Make lots of ice beforehand and keep it in big plastic bags. Compose menus well ahead and write lists accordingly, posting them up on the fridge door or noticeboard and crossing out items as you buy or make them.

Try to keep most meals simple, concentrating on the main Christmas dinner, then have a breather and plan a New Year celebration! I do hope these recipes will prove to be inspirational and help to make your Christmas really special.

Good Housekeeping Cookery Club

COOKING FOR CHRISTMAS

Maxine Clark

EBURY PRESS
LONDON

First published 1994

3 5 7 9 10 8 6 4 2

First published in the United Kingdom in 1994 by Ebury Press
Random House, 20 Vauxhall Bridge Road, London SW1V 2SA

Random House Australia (Pty) Limited
20 Alfred Street, Milsons Point, Sydney,
New South Wales 2061, Australia

Random House New Zealand Limited
18 Poland Road, Glenfield,
Auckland 10, New Zealand

Random House South Africa (Pty) Limited
PO Box 337, Bergvlei, South Africa

Random House UK Limited Reg. No. 954009

A CIP catalogue record for this book is available from the British Library.

Managing Editor: JANET ILLSLEY
Design: SARA KIDD
Special Photography: GUS FILGATE
Food Stylist: MAXINE CLARK
Photographic Stylist: ROISIN NIELD
Techniques Photography: KARL ADAMSON
Food Techniques Stylist: ANGELA KINGSBURY
Recipe Testing: EMMA-LEE GOW

ISBN 0 09 178970 2

Typeset in Gill Sans by Textype Typesetters, Cambridge
Colour Separations by Magnacraft, London
Printed and bound in Italy by New Interlitho Italia S.p.a., Milan

ICING A CHRISTMAS CAKE

The luxury Christmas cake (on page 66) makes a wonderful festive centrepiece. This step-by-step guide shows how to cover the cake with almond paste and fondant icing – to achieve a smooth finish – and how to make the decorations. Christmas cutters are available from specialist mail order suppliers (see page 80) and kitchen shops. Alternatively, make your own templates by tracing shapes from Christmas cards. Prepare decorations ahead – before you cover the cake with fondant icing – and allow to dry and harden for 1-2 days.

APPLYING THE ALMOND PASTE

1. Measure around the cake with a piece of string to give the length of almond paste required. Knead the almond paste on a surface dusted with icing sugar until pliable. Wrap one third in cling film.

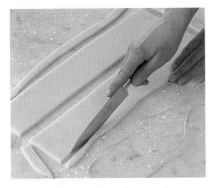

2. Dust the work surface with icing sugar. Roll the remaining two thirds of the almond paste to a rectangle slightly bigger than half of the string and twice the depth of the cake. Halve lengthways and trim to neaten.

3. Brush the side of the cake with apricot glaze. Place one piece of almond paste firmly against one side of the cake. Position the other piece to cover the other side. Smooth the joins. Roll a straight-sided jam jar around the sides to cement the almond paste to the sides.

4. Brush the top of the cake with apricot glaze. Roll the remaining almond paste to a circle to fit the top and trim to fit. Lift onto the cake with the help of a rolling pin.

5. Lightly roll the top with the rolling pin. Smooth the join and allow to dry for at least 24 hours before covering with fondant icing.

**APPLYING THE
FONDANT ICING**

1. Dust the work surface with icing sugar. Knead the icing until pliable. Roll out into a round or square 7.5 cm (3 inches) larger all round than the cake. With the help of a rolling pin, lift the icing on top of the cake and allow it to drape over the edge(s).

2. Press the icing onto the side(s) of the cake, working it down to the board. Trim off the excess.

3. Dust your fingers with a little sifted icing sugar and gently rub the surface of the cake in a circular movement to buff the icing and make it smooth.

DECORATING THE CAKE

1. To make the decorations for the starry cake, knead 450 g (1 lb) fondant icing on a surface dusted with icing sugar until pliable. Knead in 5 ml (1 tsp) gum tragacanth or dental fixative (which helps the fondant to dry and harden). Roll the fondant icing out to a thickness of 3 mm (⅛ inch).

2. Using a star-shaped cutter, stamp out about 40 stars and transfer to a baking sheet lined with non-stick baking parchment.

3. Sprinkle a little edible gold lustre powder on a plate and press some of the stars gently onto it. A little powder will stick to the surface. Place on the baking sheet and leave in a warm place for at least 24 hours to dry out and harden.

4. When dry, paint some of the plain stars with gold or silver edible food colouring.

5. If using gold leaf (see note), lightly brush a few stars with a little beaten egg white. Press the gold leaf sparingly onto the stars.

6. Arrange all of the stars around the edge of the cake as soon as it is iced if possible, pushing them lightly into the icing. Or if the icing is dry, use a little royal icing to secure them.

NOTE: If using gold leaf, it must be absolutely pure 24 carat gold, otherwise it should not be eaten. Edible gold leaf, gum tragacanth, food colourings and lustre powders are available from specialist mail order suppliers (see page 80).

VARIATIONS

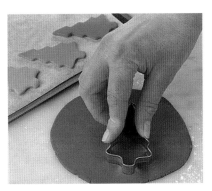

CHRISTMAS TREE DECORATION
Colour the fondant different shades of green, knead in gum tragacanth (as before) and roll out. Using a suitable cutter, stamp out about 8 Christmas trees of different shades. Leave to dry as before, then arrange standing upright as a little copse in the middle of the cake. Arrange lightly crushed white sugar lumps in piles over the cake to resemble clumps of snow. Sift icing sugar over the trees and the top of the cake.

HOLLY WREATH CAKE

1. Colour some marzipan or fondant shades of green and a little red. Using two sizes of holly leaf cutter, cut out enough leaves to make a thick wreath around the top of the cake.

2. Mark veining on each leaf, then brush the outer edge of the cake with a little beaten egg white. Arrange the leaves overlapping around the edge. Roll the red marzipan into holly berries and attach with egg white in little clumps nestling in the leaves. Tie a red bow around the cake.

GINGERBREAD NATIVITY

The gingerbread nativity (on page 76) is fun to make – especially if you have children to help you! The following step-by-step guide shows you how to make and assemble the stable, and how to decorate the figures. Use edible decorations, unless you make it known that the nativity is not to be eaten.

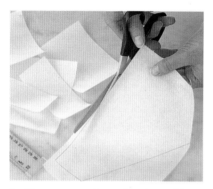

1. Cut out templates for the stable (see page 9), using greaseproof paper or cardboard. Line two baking sheets with non-stick baking parchment.

2. Roll out the larger piece of gingerbread dough to a 5 mm (¼ inch) thickness. Using the templates and a sharp knife, cut out one of each shape.

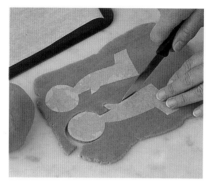

3. Trace the outlines of the figures (on pages 78-9) to make templates for Mary, Joseph, Baby Jesus, Angel Gabriel, Star of Bethlehem, Kings and Shepherds. Roll out the remaining dough and place the templates on the dough. Cut out using a sharp knife. Remember to cut 3 kings and 2-3 shepherds.

4. Carefully transfer the shapes to the baking sheets without destroying the shapes. Straighten any edges and chill for 15 minutes.

5. Bake the pieces of gingerbread in a preheated oven at 190°C (375°F) Mark 5 for 8-10 minutes or until golden brown. Leave on the baking sheet for 10 minutes, then transfer to a wire rack to cool completely.

6. Use the caramel to join the edges of the stable together and to cement it to a covered cake board. Dip the edges in the caramel and push them together or use a spoon to coat the edges. Remelt the caramel as necessary by sitting the pan in a saucepan of boiling water until it liquifies again. Join the roof to the stable with the caramel.

7. Stick twiglets or clean straw matting to the roof, or leave plain if preferred. Scatter different shades of sugar around the stable to resemble sand and earth.

9. Decorate the characters with glacé or royal icing. Allow to dry before assembling in and around the stable.

10. Cement a toffee or flat sweet to the base of each figure with a little icing or caramel so that it will stand upright. Stick suitable sweets onto the Kings to resemble their gifts.

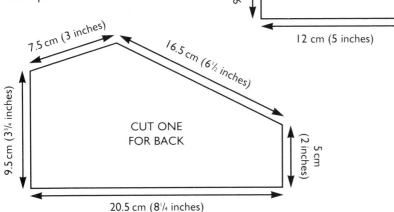

8. Give Baby Jesus, Mary, Joseph and the Angel gold halos, and the Kings and Star of Bethlehem a bit of gold too! Stick gold leaf on with a little beaten egg white or apply gold lustre powder.

STABLE TEMPLATES

CUT ONE
FOR SIDE

5 cm
(2 inches)

12 cm (5 inches)

CUT ONE
FOR SIDE

9.5 cm (3¾ inches)

12 cm (5 inches)

CUT ONE
FOR ROOF

18 cm (7 inches)

13.5 cm (5½ inches)
including overhang

CUT ONE
FOR BACK

7.5 cm (3 inches)

16.5 cm (6½ inches)

9.5 cm (3¾ inches)

5 cm
(2 inches)

20.5 cm (8¼ inches)

CUT ONE
FOR ROOF

9 cm (3½ inches)
including overhang

13.5 cm (5½ inches)
including overhang

PICKLED SALMON ON RYE

This homemade 'gravad lax' incorporates a dash of teriyaki marinade and a little fresh ginger to give it a Japanese overtone. Slice it vertically and quite thickly – like sashimi – and serve on rounds of dark rye bread or pumpernickel spread with a little horseradish mixed with ginger. As this pickled salmon keeps well in the fridge, the recipe uses a whole filleted salmon – sufficient for 6-8 as a starter, plus enough for a drinks party.

SERVES 12-15

1 salmon, about 1.4 kg
  (3 lb), filleted and
  trimmed, but not skinned
15 ml (1 tbsp) sunflower oil
1 cm (½ inch) piece fresh
  root ginger
30 ml (2 tbsp) sugar
15 ml (1 tbsp) coarse sea salt
30-45 ml (2-3 tbsp) white
  peppercorns, crushed
15 ml (1 tbsp) vodka or rice
  wine (saki)
15 ml (1 tbsp) teriyaki
  marinade (eg Kikkoman's)
SAUCE
30 ml (2 tbsp) horseradish
  sauce (or milder creamed
  horseradish)
1 cm (½ inch) piece fresh
  root ginger
TO SERVE
thinly sliced rye bread or
  pumpernickel
salad leaves
snipped chives, to garnish

PREPARATION TIME
20 minutes, plus marinating
COOKING TIME
Nil
FREEZING
Suitable

175-140 CALS PER SERVING

1. Remove any small bones from the salmon with tweezers. Rub the flesh with the oil.

2. Peel and finely chop the ginger and mix with the sugar, salt and crushed peppercorns.

3. Lay one salmon fillet, skin-side down, on a large sheet of greaseproof paper on top of a sheet of kitchen foil. Spread the spice mixture evenly over the flesh. Moisten with the vodka and teriyaki marinade.

4. Lay the other fillet on top and wrap the whole 'sandwich' up tightly in the paper, then foil. Lay in a non-corrosive dish and cover with a small tray. Place a 450 g (1 lb) weight on top. Leave at cool room temperature for 4 hours.

5. After 4 hours, turn the parcel over and replace the tray and weight. Leave at cool room temperature for a further 4 hours, then remove the weight and refrigerate for 4 hours. The salmon will be ready to eat after this time, but the longer it sits in the marinade, the stronger the flavour will become (see note).

6. For the sauce, put the horseradish sauce in a small bowl. Peel and chop the ginger and squeeze through a garlic press into the horseradish sauce.

7. Unwrap the salmon parcel, retaining the juices, and scrape off the excess peppercorns. Slice the salmon vertically, into 5 mm (¼ inch) thick slices, then cut horizontally, close to the skin, to release each slice.

8. Spread a little sauce on each slice of rye bread. Arrange the pickled salmon slices on the bread. Serve with a little salad, a drizzle of marinade and a sprinkling of chives.

NOTE: Keep salmon tightly wrapped with the juices, and slice as you need it.

TECHNIQUE

Sandwich the salmon fillets together with the spice mixture, moistened with the vodka and marinade.

Marinated Olives and Spiced Nuts

Make these perfumed olives at least a month before Christmas to allow the olives to fully absorb the flavours. Serve with drinks or layer in small pots to use as gifts. The deliciously spicy nuts are wonderful served almost straight from the oven while still warm. Alternatively cool them and store in an airtight tin for up to 2 weeks – any longer and they go stale.

MAKES 450 G (1 LB) EACH

OLIVES
200 g (7 oz) each black, green and stuffed olives
30 ml (2 tbsp) coriander seeds
finely pared rind of 1 orange, shredded
few fresh coriander sprigs
450-750 ml (¾-1¼ pints) extra-virgin olive oil (depending on size of jar)

NUTS
350 g (12 oz) mixed skinned nuts, such as almonds, pecans, hazelnuts
125 g (4 oz) shelled mixed pumpkin and sunflower seeds
40 g (1½ oz) butter or 45 ml (3 tbsp) sunflower oil
15 ml (1 tbsp) curry powder or garam masala
5 ml (1 tsp) coarse sea salt

PREPARATION TIME
20 minutes, plus marinating olives
COOKING TIME
Nuts: 30 minutes
FREEZING
Not suitable

1. Using a rolling pin, lightly hit each black and green olive to split without crushing completely. Alternatively, slit with a small sharp knife. (Stoned olives do not need cracking).

2. Arrange the black, green and stuffed olives in layers in an attractive 1.2 litre (2 pint) glass jar. Sprinkle each layer with coriander seeds and orange rind shreds. Tuck a few sprigs of coriander down the side of the jar.

3. Warm the olive oil in a saucepan to release the aroma, then pour sufficient into the jar to cover the olives completely. Tapping the jar to release any air bubbles, seal tightly and allow to cool. Leave in a cool dark place for 1 month to mature.

4. To prepare the nuts, preheat the oven to 150°C (300°F) Mark 2. Melt the butter in a roasting tin and stir in the curry powder. Cook, stirring, for 30 seconds. Add the nuts and seeds and stir until well coated.

5. Roast in the oven for 30 minutes, stirring from time to time. On removing from the oven, immediately toss the nuts with the salt. Serve warm, or allow to cool completely and store for up to 2 weeks.

NOTE: The nicest stuffed olives are those filled with anchovies or almonds.

CALORIE COUNTS: Per 25 g (1 oz), the olives provide 50 cals; the nuts provide 195 cals.

VARIATION

For an oriental accent, flavour the nuts with 10 ml (2 tsp) Chinese five-spice powder instead of the curry powder.

TECHNIQUE

Layer the different olives in a jar, sprinkling each layer with coriander seeds and orange rind.

HAM AND HERB TERRINE

Parma ham and freshly chopped mixed herbs add a subtle sweetness to this version of the renowned *jambon persillé* from Burgundy in France. It makes a very good starter or buffet dish as it keeps well for a few days in the refrigerator – the flavour even improves with keeping!

SERVES 6-8

1.1 kg (2½ lb) piece
  unsmoked gammon
1 bouquet garni
6 black peppercorns
1 onion, peeled
1 leek, trimmed
1 celery stick
1 carrot, peeled
300 ml (½ pint) dry white
  wine
6 good thin slices of Parma
  ham or prosciutto, plus an
  extra 125 g (4 oz)
salt and pepper
30 ml (2 tbsp) wholegrain
  mustard
25 g (1 oz) powdered
  gelatine
90 ml (6 tbsp) chopped
  mixed fresh herbs
  (parsley, tarragon, chives)
salad leaves, to garnish

PREPARATION TIME
35 minutes, plus overnight
soaking
COOKING TIME
About 1½ hours
FREEZING
Suitable: For up to 3 months

450-340 CALS PER SERVING

1. Place the ham in a large pot or bowl, cover with cold water and leave to soak overnight to draw out excess salt.

2. Pour off the water and rinse the ham. Return to the pan. Add the bouquet garni, peppercorns, onion, leek, celery, carrot, wine and enough water to cover. Slowly bring to the boil, skim, then simmer very gently for 1½ hours or until the ham is very tender. Keep skimming throughout cooking to ensure a clear stock. Allow to cool for 10 minutes.

3. Meanwhile line a 1.2 litre (2 pint) mould with overlapping slices of Parma ham. Shred the 125 g (4 oz) Parma ham.

4. Take the meat out of the liquid. Cut off and discard the fat and skin. Using two forks, tear the meat into large chunks and mix with the Parma ham. Pile into the lined mould.

5. Strain the stock through a fine sieve or through a sieve lined with kitchen paper into a measuring jug – you should have at least 900 ml (1½ pints). Leave to cool, then chill – the fat will rise to the surface and set on top.

6. Remove the layer of fat and pour the stock into a saucepan. Boil rapidly to reduce to 900 ml (1½ pints) if necessary. Taste and season the stock. Stir in the mustard. Sprinkle the gelatine over the surface of the hot stock and stir in until

dissolved. Remove from the heat and stir in the chopped herbs. Cool until syrupy, then pour sufficient stock over the ham in the terrine to cover it. Tap the terrine on the surface to dislodge any trapped air bubbles. Chill for at least 2 hours until set.

7. To unmould, dip briefly in warm water and turn out onto a serving dish. Cut into thick slices and garnish with salad leaves. Accompany with a caper and gherkin relish if desired.

TECHNIQUE

Pour the jellied stock over the ham in the terrine to cover completely. Depending on the shape of the terrine, you may not need to use all of it.

SMOKED FISH PÂTÉ WITH MELBA TOAST

A pretty, chunky, smoked fish mousse combining pale pink trout with flakes of white smoked cod. Try other combinations such as kipper with smoked haddock, or Scottish smokie (hot-smoked haddock) with cubes of smoked salmon for real luxury!

SERVES 4-6

125 g (4 oz) smoked cod
2 large hot-smoked pink
    trout (in skins), each
    about 200 g (7 oz)
150 ml (¼ pint) soured
    cream
150 ml (¼ pint) fromage
    frais
2.5 ml (½ tsp) hot paprika
lemon juice, to taste
salt and pepper
MELBA TOAST
3-4 slices day-old softgrain
    white bread
TO GARNISH
paprika, for sprinkling

PREPARATION TIME
20 minutes, plus chilling
COOKING TIME
5 minutes
FREEZING
Not suitable

365-245 CALS PER SERVING

1. Place the smoked cod, skin uppermost, in a pan and cover with water. Simmer for 5 minutes until the fish is opaque and flakes easily. Lift out the fish, remove the skin and flake roughly. Set aside in a bowl to cool.

2. Peel the skin from the trout and flake the flesh into a food processor or blender. Add the soured cream, fromage frais and paprika; process until smooth. Taste and add lemon juice, salt and pepper to taste.

3. Scrape the trout out into the bowl containing the cod and mix gently but thoroughly, taking care to avoid breaking up the flakes of cod. Spoon into a serving dish or individual dishes and smooth the tops. Chill in the refrigerator for at least 3 hours.

4. Meanwhile, make the Melba toast. Preheat the oven to 180°C (350°F) Mark 4. Toast the bread lightly on both sides. Quickly cut off the crusts and split each slice in two. Scrape off any doughy bits. Place on a baking sheet and bake in the oven for 10-15 minutes or until uniformly golden.

5. Serve the smoked fish pâté sprinkled with a little paprika and accompanied by the hot Melba toast.

NOTE: For convenience the Melba toast can be prepared well ahead, then cooled and stored in an airtight tin. Warm through in a moderate oven just before serving.

TECHNIQUE

Using two forks, divide the poached smoked cod into flakes.

CARROT, CHESTNUT AND CORIANDER SOUP

A chunky orange and green winter soup made with homemade stock and flavoured with coriander for a really intense, warming flavour. At this time of year it is worth making a big pot of good stock for soups, sauces and gravies – keep a supply in the freezer. Serve this nourishing soup with hot herb bread.

SERVES 6-8

CHICKEN STOCK

2 onions

2 cloves

3 carrots

2 celery sticks, with leaves

1 raw or cooked chicken
  carcass, plus giblets

2-3 parsley sprigs

1 bouquet garni

1 bay leaf

6 black peppercorns

SOUP

450 g (1 lb) fresh chestnuts
  (see note)

900 g (2 lb) carrots

2 medium leeks

50 g (2 oz) butter

15 ml (1 tbsp) ground
  coriander

pinch of sugar

60 ml (4 tbsp) chopped fresh
  coriander

salt and pepper

PREPARATION TIME
25 minutes
COOKING TIME
1½ hours
FREEZING
Suitable

255-190 CALS PER SERVING

1. To make the stock, halve the unpeeled onions vertically and stud with the cloves. Chop the carrots roughly without peeling. Roughly chop the celery. Place all the vegetables in a large saucepan with the chicken carcass, giblets if available (excluding liver), herbs and spices. Cover with at least 2 litres (3½ pints) cold water and bring slowly to the boil, skimming off any scum that rises to the surface. Reduce the heat, half-cover and simmer for at least 1 hour. Strain the stock through a fine sieve and discard the chicken and vegetables. Cool, then remove any fat from the surface.

2. For the soup, pierce the flat sides of the chestnuts and immerse in a pan of boiling water for 5 minutes. Drain and peel when cool enough to handle. Chop roughly and reserve.

3. Peel the carrots then cut into medium chunks. Trim and slice the leeks into rounds.

4. Melt the butter in a saucepan and add half of the carrots, all of the leeks and the ground coriander. Cook gently for about 5 minutes until softened, then add 1.7 litres (3 pints) stock and the sugar. Half-cover and simmer for 20 minutes until the vegetables are very tender.

5. Meanwhile, cook the reserved carrots in a steamer or boiling salted water for 15-20 minutes until tender. Set aside.

6. Purée the soup in a blender or food processor until smooth, then return to the pan. Stir in the reserved carrots, chestnuts and fresh coriander. Check the seasoning. Reheat until almost boiling.

7. Pour into warmed soup bowls and serve with hot herb bread.

NOTE: If you cannot get hold of fresh chestnuts, vacuum-packed chestnuts are a good alternative. They need no preparation. You will need a 350 g (12 oz) pack.

TECHNIQUE

Add the chopped fresh coriander to the puréed soup, with the cooked carrot chunks and chestnuts.

ROAST STUFFED TURKEY

This roasting method ensures that the bird remains moist and the skin beautifully brown and crisp. Try to use a fresh rather than a thoroughly defrosted frozen turkey – the flavour is much better, and less water emerges during cooking. Free-range bronze turkeys are particularly flavoursome. Stuff the turkey just before roasting.

SERVES 8 (plus leftovers)

4.5-5.5 kg (10-12 lb) turkey
175-225 g (6-8 oz) butter,
    softened
salt and pepper
LEEK STUFFING
450 g (1 lb) fresh spinach,
    stalks removed, or 225 g
    (8 oz) frozen chopped
    spinach, thawed
450 g (1 lb) leeks
50 g (2 oz) butter
1 garlic clove, crushed
225 g (8 oz) cooked multi-
    grain rice (eg Countrywild)
25 g (1 oz) pine nuts,
    toasted
45 ml (3 tbsp) chopped
    mixed fresh herbs
freshly grated nutmeg
1 egg
SAUSAGE STUFFING
350 g (12 oz) spicy Italian
    pork sausages, skinned
2 onions, peeled
125 g (4 oz) butter
225 g (8 oz) oatmeal
5 ml (1 tsp) chopped thyme

PREPARATION TIME
45 minutes
COOKING TIME
3½-5 hours, plus resting
FREEZING
Suitable: Stuffings only

645 CALS PER SERVING

1. Remove giblets from turkey, discard liver and use the rest to make stock for gravy. Place in a saucepan with flavouring ingredients (1 halved onion, 1 chopped carrot, few parsley sprigs, 1 bay leaf and a few black peppercorns). Cover with at least 600 ml (1 pint) water, bring to the boil, then simmer for 1 hour. Strain.

2. To prepare the stuffings, wash the fresh spinach and cook in a covered pan, with just the water that still clings to the leaves, until just wilted. Drain, squeeze out excess moisture and chop roughly. If using frozen spinach, just squeeze dry. Trim and chop the leeks. Melt the butter in a frying pan, add the leeks and garlic and cook gently until soft. Stir in the spinach, rice, nuts and herbs. Season liberally with nutmeg, salt and pepper. Bind with the egg. Allow to cool.

3. To make the sausage stuffing, break up the sausages in a bowl. Chop the onions and sauté in the butter until soft and golden, then mix in the oatmeal and thyme. Add to the sausagemeat and mix thoroughly. Season well and let cool.

4. Preheat the oven to 180°C (350°F) Mark 4. Wash the bird thoroughly inside and out; dry with kitchen paper. Use one stuffing to stuff the neck flap (cook the other in a separate dish). Spread butter over turkey and season well. Weigh bird and calculate cooking time: allow 20 minutes per 450 g (1 lb), plus 20 minutes extra.

5. Line a large roasting tin with foil, bringing the edges over the rim. Place the turkey in the centre, covering it loosely with another sheet of foil, tucking the edges inside the rim. Roast for the calculated cooking time, removing the covering foil for the last 30 minutes to brown. Test the deepest part of each thigh with a skewer to check that the juices run clear and the bird is cooked through. Transfer to a platter, cover and rest in a warm place for 15 minutes.

6. Skim off the fat from the roasting juices, reserving 45 ml (3 tbsp). Add the juices to the stock. Heat the reserved fat in a saucepan and stir in 15 ml (1 tbsp) flour. Whisk in the stock and bring to the boil. Simmer for 5 minutes, season and strain into a warm sauceboat.

7. Serve the turkey with the gravy and traditional accompaniments.

TECHNIQUE

Stuff the neck of the bird and secure with a skewer or sew up with cotton string.

FRENCH ROAST PHEASANT WITH GRAPES AND NUTS

Tender moist pheasants are glazed with clementine juice, crushed grapes and Madeira and roasted to perfection. The liquids in the pan stop the pheasant drying out – especially if you baste during cooking. The pan juices are then used to make a rich and luxurious sauce that's Russian in inspiration.

SERVES 6

6 clementines

700 g (1½ lb) white or red grapes

40 fresh walnuts in shell, or 225 g (8 oz) walnut halves

15 ml (1 tbsp) green tea (Gunpowder or Darjeeling)

200 ml (7 fl oz) Madeira or sweet sherry

2 young pheasants, plucked, drawn and trussed with giblets (see note)

softened butter, for basting

salt and pepper

10 ml (2 tsp) balsamic or sherry vinegar

15 ml (1 tbsp) dark soy sauce

TO GARNISH

extra grapes

pheasant feathers, if available

PREPARATION TIME
45 minutes
COOKING TIME
45 minutes
FREEZING
Not suitable

635 CALS PER SERVING

1. Preheat the oven to 200°C (400°F) Mark 6. Grate the rind from 2 clementines and squeeze the juice from all six; place in a bowl. Reserve the ungrated squeezed halves. Whizz the grapes roughly in a food processor and pour into the clementine juice. Shell the fresh walnuts. Pour 300 ml (½ pint) boiling water over the green tea, leave to steep for 5 minutes, then strain and reserve.

2. Pour half the clementine and grape juice into a roasting tin, adding the Madeira and any giblets (except the liver). Place the reserved clementine halves inside the pheasant cavities. Smear the pheasants with butter and season with salt and pepper.

3. Place the birds in the roasting tin on one side, leg uppermost. Roast in the oven for 15 minutes. Turn the birds over on the other side, baste with the pan juices and roast for another 15 minutes. Finally sit the birds upright, baste well and roast for a final 15 minutes or until done. Test by pushing a skewer into the meatiest part of the thigh; the juices should run clear. Transfer the pheasants to a warmed serving platter and keep warm.

4. Pour the reserved clementine and grape juice into the roasting tin. Stir in the tea, balsamic vinegar and soy sauce.

Place over the heat and bring to the boil, scraping up any sediment from the bottom of the pan. Boil for 1-2 minutes, then strain into a saucepan, pressing the juice through the sieve with the back of a wooden spoon. Stir in the walnuts, bring to the boil and reduce to 450 ml (¾ pint). Taste and season well. The sauce should be slightly syrupy; if not, reduce a little more. Spoon the walnuts around the pheasant and pour the sauce into a warmed sauceboat.

5. Dress the pheasant with grapes and cleaned pheasant feathers, if available. Serve with the sauce.

NOTE: If your butcher is preparing the birds, ask him to keep the feathers and giblets. Or use chicken or turkey giblets.

TECHNIQUE

Baste the pheasants with the pan juices as you turn them, to keep them moist.

TURKEY POT PIE

This tempting supper dish is loosely based on an American recipe in which the 'pie' is topped with 'biscuits' or cobblers to make a homely crust. It is an excellent way of using up turkey and ham leftovers – combining them in a delicious creamy sauce. You will need a chunky piece of ham.

SERVES 6-8

700 g (1½ lb) cooked
    boneless turkey
225 g (8 oz) cooked ham
2 carrots
1 large leek
125 g (4 oz) baby corn cobs
225 g (8 oz) chestnut or
    button mushrooms
900 ml (1½ pints) chicken
    stock
150 ml (¼ pint) dry white
    wine
1 bay leaf
2 fresh rosemary sprigs
75 g (3 oz) butter
60 ml (4 tbsp) plain flour
300 ml (½ pint) single cream
salt and pepper
HERB COBBLERS
350 g (12 oz) self-raising flour
30 ml (2 tbsp) chopped parsley
30 ml (2 tbsp) chopped chives
75 g (3 oz) butter
about 200 ml (7 fl oz) milk
TO GARNISH
coarse sea salt
rosemary leaves

PREPARATION TIME
40 minutes
COOKING TIME
40 minutes
FREEZING
Suitable: Stage 7

735-550 CALS PER SERVING

1. Cut the turkey into bite-sized pieces. Cut the ham into large cubes. Place the meat in a 1.7 litre (3 pint) ovenproof dish.

2. Peel and cut the carrots into thick sticks. Thickly slice the leek. Halve the baby corn. Quarter the mushrooms.

3. Pour the stock into a saucepan and add the wine, bay leaf and rosemary. Bring to the boil, add the carrots and cook for 10 minutes. Add the leeks and baby corn and cook for 5-8 minutes until all of the vegetables are tender. Strain the stock into a jug; set the vegetables aside.

4. Melt the butter in a saucepan, add the mushrooms and cook until beginning to colour. Sprinkle in the flour. Take off the heat and mix well. Stir in the stock and cream. Return to the heat and slowly bring to the boil, stirring all the time. Simmer for 5 minutes, taste and season. Cover the surface closely with dampened greaseproof paper, to prevent a skin forming, and allow to cool.

5. Preheat the oven to 220°C (425°F) Mark 7. To make the herb cobblers, sift the flour with 2.5 ml (½ tsp) salt into a bowl and stir in the chopped herbs. Rub in the butter until the mixture resembles fine breadcrumbs. Stir in enough milk to make a soft scone dough. (Alternatively, you can prepare the dough in a food processor.) Turn out onto a floured surface and knead lightly.

6. Roll out the dough to a 1 cm (½ inch) thickness and cut out at least nine 7.5 cm (3 inch) squares with a sharp knife. Halve these diagonally to make triangles.

7. Add the vegetables and sauce to the meat and mix well. Arrange the herb cobblers, overlapping, around the edge of the dish and sprinkle with coarse sea salt.

8. Bake in the oven for 10 minutes until the cobblers are risen and browning, then lower the temperature to 190°C (375°F) Mark 5. Bake for 15 minutes, then brush with milk again and sprinkle with about 15 ml (1 tbsp) rosemary leaves. Bake for a further 15 minutes. Serve piping hot, with a green vegetable.

NOTE: If fresh chives or parsley are unavailable, use freeze-dried herbs but halve the quantities.

TECHNIQUE

To shape the herb cobblers, cut the rolled-out dough into 7.5 cm (3 inch) squares, then halve these to make triangles.

ROAST RIB OF BEEF WITH CHESTNUT RELISH

This is perfect for an alternative Christmas dinner or a Hogmanay supper or New Year's Day lunch, especially if you are feeding large numbers. Ask the butcher for a well-hung piece of Aberdeen Angus or real Scottish beef – the flavour of the meat will speak for itself. The only adornment is a sweet sour relish of shallots, pickled walnuts and fresh chestnuts – which should be made the day before to allow the flavours to mature.

SERVES 8

2.3 kg (5 lb) prime rib or
   sirloin roast
coarse sea salt and pepper
PICKLED RELISH
900 g (2 lb) shallots
450 g (1 lb) fresh chestnuts,
   or 350 g (12 oz) vacuum-
   packed ones
8 pickled walnuts, drained
150 g (5 oz) butter
175 g (6 oz) soft light brown
   sugar
30 ml (2 tbsp) each balsamic
   and sherry vinegars
300 ml (½ pint) medium dry
   white wine
RICH WINE GRAVY
1 bottle full-bodied red wine
1 onion, peeled and sliced
30 ml (2 tbsp) plain flour
1 litre (1¾ pints) good
   concentrated beef stock

PREPARATION TIME
45 minutes
COOKING TIME
About 1½-2¼ hours
FREEZING
Not suitable

655 CALS PER SERVING

1. To make the relish, cover the shallots with boiling water, leave for 5 minutes, then peel and slice. Pierce the flat side of each chestnut and immerse in boiling water for 5 minutes. Drain, peel and chop roughly. Roughly chop the walnuts.

2. Melt the butter in a saucepan and cook until a light brown. Stir in the shallots and sugar; season well. Cover and cook very slowly for 30 minutes, stirring occasionally, until soft and evenly caramelised. Stir in the vinegars and wine and cook briskly, stirring occasionally, for 15 minutes or until well reduced. Stir in the chestnuts and walnuts and cook for 5 minutes. Check the seasoning. Cool, cover and leave to stand overnight.

3. Let the beef come to room temperature. Preheat the oven to 180°C (350°F) Mark 4. Weigh the beef and calculate the cooking time: allow 17 minutes per 450 g (1 lb) for rare; 24 minutes for medium; 27 minutes well done.

4. Lay beef fat-side up in a roasting tin and rub with coarse salt and pepper. Roast in the oven for the calculated cooking time.

5. Meanwhile pour the wine into a frying pan and boil to reduce down to 150 ml (¼ pint); it will be dark and syrupy.

6. Remove the beef from the oven, cover loosely and let stand in a warm place for 15 minutes.

7. Skim off excess fat from the juices in the roasting tin. Add the onion and cook for 2-3 minutes. Sprinkle in the flour, stir well and cook for 5 minutes until browning. Whisk in the stock and reduced wine, bring to the boil and simmer for 10 minutes. Check the seasoning. Strain into a warm gravy boat.

8. Reheat the relish and transfer to a warmed serving bowl. Set the beef on a heated platter and surround with bay leaves and rosemary sprigs. Serve with the relish, gravy, seasonal vegetables, roast potatoes and Yorkshire puddings.

TECHNIQUE

For the relish, cook the shallots slowly until evenly browned and caramelised.

GLAZED PORK LOIN WITH FIG STUFFING

A tender loin of pork rolled around a tasty fig, apple and rosemary stuffing, then roasted until the crackling is a deep mahogany brown and deliciously crisp. It is important to score the crackling deeply to ensure a crisp result. The crackling bastes the meat during cooking and keeps it moist.

SERVES 6

1.4 kg (3 lb) boned loin of
  pork, skin well scored
salt and pepper
FIG STUFFING
4 shallots
1 garlic clove
225 g (8 oz) no-need-to-soak
  dried figs
1 eating apple
2 fresh rosemary sprigs
50 g (2 oz) butter
finely grated rind and juice
  of 1 lemon
45 ml (3 tbsp) dry sherry
GLAZE
60 ml (4 tbsp) thin honey
10 ml (2 tsp) mustard
  powder
finely grated rind of 1 lemon
TO GARNISH
rosemary sprigs
few fresh figs

PREPARATION TIME
30 minutes
COOKING TIME
2 hours
FREEZING
Not suitable

480 CALS PER SERVING

1. For the stuffing, peel and finely chop the shallots. Crush the garlic. Roughly chop the figs. Peel, core and finely chop the apple. Chop the rosemary.

2. Melt the butter in a saucepan and add the shallots and garlic. Cook for 5-10 minutes until soft and golden. Stir in the figs, apple, rosemary, lemon rind and juice, and sherry. Cook, stirring, for 5 minutes until slightly softened and most of the liquid has evaporated. Cool.

3. Preheat the oven to 190°C (375°F) Mark 5. Lay the pork loin, skin-side down, on a clean surface. Season well with salt and pepper and spread the stuffing along the middle. Roll up and tie at intervals with fine string. Place in a roasting tin and roast in the oven for 1 hour.

4. Meanwhile, make the glaze. Place the honey, mustard and lemon rind in a saucepan and heat gently, stirring. Brush over the pork skin and roast for a further 45 minutes, basting every 15 minutes with the glaze.

5. Leave the meat to rest in a warm place for 15 minutes. Carve into thick slices and serve garnished with sprigs of rosemary. Accompany with a gravy made from the pan juices if wished, and seasonal vegetables.

NOTE: If you buy a pork loin without crackling, brown it all over in butter after stuffing, before roasting.

Any leftover stuffing can be used to fill halved and cored eating apples. Roast around the joint for the last 20 minutes and serve as an accompaniment.

VARIATION

Replace the figs with no-need-to-soak stoned prunes or apricots. Use thyme instead of rosemary.

TECHNIQUE

Tie the stuffed pork loin at regular intervals with fine cotton string to secure the stuffing.

BRAISED HAM WITH MADEIRA MUSTARD SAUCE

This beautiful ham braised in Madeira is served with a piquant creamy mustard sauce, made with the cooking juices. It is large enough to serve 6-8 as a hot main course and leave sufficient to serve cold over the festive holiday. If preferred, you could of course buy a smaller joint.

SERVES 12-16

3.7 kg (6 lb) piece of gammon
½ bottle medium white wine
6 cloves
8 peppercorns
½ bottle Madeira
SAUCE
8 shallots
300 ml (½ pint) dry white wine
about 300 ml (½ pint) light stock
75 g (3 oz) butter
40 g (1½ oz) plain flour
6 juniper berries, crushed
6 dried green peppercorns, crushed
120 ml (4 fl oz) white wine vinegar
30 ml (2 tbsp) Dijon mustard
120 ml (4 fl oz) crème fraîche or soured cream
salt and pepper

PREPARATION TIME
30 minutes, plus overnight soaking
COOKING TIME
About 3¼-3½ hours
FREEZING
Suitable: Sauce only

625-515 CALS PER SERVING

1. Cover the gammon with cold water and leave to soak overnight. Scrub the skin and drain and dry well. Weigh the gammon and calculate the poaching time, allowing 25 minutes per 450 g (1 lb).

2. Place the gammon in a large pan and cover with cold water. Bring slowly to the boil, then drain off the water. Pour the wine into the pan and add the cloves and peppercorns and enough hot water to cover. Cover and simmer very gently for the calculated time. Allow the gammon to cool in the liquid, then drain.

3. Preheat the oven to 180°C (350°F) Mark 4. Strip the rind off the gammon and score the fat into a diamond pattern. Place the gammon in a roasting tin and pour over the Madeira. Braise in the oven for 45 minutes to 1 hour, basting frequently, until golden brown.

4. Meanwhile, peel and chop the shallots. Transfer the gammon to a platter, cover loosely and keep warm while making the sauce.

5. Pour off the juices from the roasting tin into a measuring jug and wait for the fat to rise to the surface. Skim off the fat and reserve 30 ml (2 tbsp). Make the braising liquid up to 1.2 litres (2 pints) with the wine and stock.

6. Melt the butter and reserved ham fat in a saucepan. Add the flour and cook, stirring, for 3-4 minutes until foaming. Whisk in the wine and stock mixture. Add the juniper berries and half the shallots. Bring to the boil and simmer for 10 minutes.

7. Meanwhile, put the green peppercorns, remaining shallots and vinegar in a saucepan and reduce to 10 ml (2 tsp). Dip the base of the pan into cold water to stop the reduction. Stir the Madeira sauce into the reduced vinegar with the mustard and simmer for at least 15 minutes. Stir in the crème fraîche or cream and bring to the boil. Check the seasoning. Pour into a warmed sauceboat.

8. Slice the ham and serve with the sauce and seasonal vegetables.

TECHNIQUE

Before braising, score the gammon fat in a diamond pattern, using a sharp knife.

BAKED SALMON WITH EASY SAFFRON HOLLANDAISE

A whole fish is a magnificent centrepiece for any gathering or celebration. Ask the fishmonger to gut the fish for you. And make sure that you have a large enough baking tin – you can always bend the salmon into a curve to fit the tin! The saffron hollandaise has a delicate piquant taste and a vivid yellow colour.

SERVES 6-8

melted butter, for brushing
salt and pepper
1 salmon, about 2 kg
   (4½ lb), cleaned
1 Florence fennel bulb
6 spring onions
finely pared rind of 1 lemon
6 fresh tarragon sprigs, or
   30 ml (2 tbsp) freeze-dried
150 ml (¼ pint) dry
   vermouth
SAFFRON HOLLANDAISE
5 ml (1 tsp) saffron threads,
   or 1 small packet
   powdered saffron
150 ml (¼ pint) dry
   vermouth
30 ml (2 tbsp) tarragon
   vinegar
6 egg yolks
350 g (12 oz) unsalted butter
TO GARNISH
herb sprigs
lemon slices (optional)

PREPARATION TIME
20 minutes
COOKING TIME
1 hour
FREEZING
Not suitable

720-450 CALS PER SERVING

1. Preheat the oven to 140°C (275°F) Mark 1. Take a sheet of foil – large enough to loosely wrap the salmon – and place in a baking tin. Brush liberally with melted butter and season with salt and pepper. Tear two long strips of foil and lay these across the sheet of foil to help lift the fish.

2. Lay the fish in the middle of the foil with the two strips underneath. Slice the fennel and spring onions. Tuck these inside the cavity with the lemon rind and tarragon. Sprinkle the vermouth over the salmon and season well.

3. Wrap the salmon loosely but securely in the foil, making sure that no steam can escape. Bake in the oven for 1 hour. Test by opening the parcel and piercing the fish to the bone at the thickest part – it should be opaque and flake easily. If not, re-wrap and cook for another 10 minutes or until done.

4. To make the hollandaise, heat the saffron, vermouth and vinegar together, then leave to stand for 15 minutes. Place the egg yolks in a blender or food processor and blend for 30 seconds. Melt the butter in a saucepan.

5. Bring the vermouth mixture to the boil and boil rapidly until reduced to

about 45 ml (3 tbsp). Heat the butter until boiling then, with the blender or food processor running, immediately and slowly pour onto the egg yolks. The mixture should immediately thicken to a coating consistency. Pour in the reduced vermouth and process for 10 seconds. Pour into a warmed heatproof jug and stand in a bowl of warm water until ready to serve. (The water must not be too hot or the sauce will curdle.)

6. Remove the fish from the oven and unwrap. Lift out, using the foil strips, onto a warmed serving dish. Remove the foil strips and quickly garnish the salmon with herbs, and lemon slices if wished. Serve immediately, accompanied by the saffron hollandaise.

TECHNIQUE

For the hollandaise, pour the boiling butter in a slow steady stream onto the egg yolks, with the machine running.

VEGETABLE RAGOÛT WITH CHEESE POLENTA TOPPING

A rich, thick stew of leeks, tomatoes, aubergines and chick peas, topped with a golden crust of cheesy, herby polenta. It will appeal to meat eaters and vegetarians alike, and is a perfect hot buffet dish which can be cooked ahead for larger numbers.

SERVES 6-8

700 g (1½ lb) aubergines
salt and pepper
450 g (1 lb) leeks
450 g (1 lb) ripe red
   tomatoes
150 ml (¼ pint) olive oil
2 garlic cloves, crushed
150 ml (¼ pint) dry white
   wine
400 g (14 oz) can chopped
   tomatoes
30 ml (2 tbsp) sun-dried
   tomato paste
400 g (14 oz) can chick peas

POLENTA TOPPING

375 g (13 oz) packet quick-
   cook polenta
125 g (4 oz) Gruyère cheese,
   grated
90 ml (6 tbsp) freshly grated
   Parmesan cheese
15 ml (1 tbsp) dried mixed
   Provençal herbs (or fresh
   herbs if available)

PREPARATION TIME
40 minutes, plus cooling
COOKING TIME
30 minutes
FREEZING
Suitable: Stage 7

750-560 CALS PER SERVING

1. Cut the aubergines into large chunks, place in a colander and sprinkle with salt. Leave to drain for 30 minutes.

2. Wash and trim the leeks, then slice thickly. Plunge the tomatoes into boiling water for 30 seconds. Refresh under cold water and slip off the skins. Halve, squeeze out the seeds and discard. Cut the tomatoes into quarters.

3. Heat 30 ml (2 tbsp) olive oil in a large pan and add the leeks and garlic. Fry over a medium heat for 5 minutes until softened and beginning to brown, but not disintegrate.

4. Add the fresh tomatoes and wine and cook over a high heat for about 7 minutes until the tomatoes have softened and the wine has evaporated. Stir in the canned tomatoes, tomato paste and drained chick peas.

5. Rinse the aubergines thoroughly, then pat dry with kitchen paper. Heat the remaining olive oil in a frying pan and fry the aubergines over a high heat until browning. Stir into the leek and tomato mixture. Pour into a large shallow oven-proof dish and allow to cool.

6. Bring 1.6 litres (2¾ pints) water to the boil in a large heavy-based pan, with

10 ml (2 tsp) salt added. Sprinkle in the polenta, stirring all the time. Cook, stirring, for 5-10 minutes until thick. Stir in the Gruyère, 60 ml (4 tbsp) Parmesan cheese, plenty of seasoning and the herbs. Spread in a shallow tin to a thickness of 2 cm (¾ inch) and allow to cool. When cold, stamp into rounds with a 4 cm (1½ inch) plain cutter.

7. Preheat the oven to 200°C (400°F) Mark 6. Arrange the polenta in overlapping circles around the dish, leaving a space in the middle.

8. Sprinkle with extra Parmesan cheese and bake for about 30 minutes until golden brown and heated through. Serve immediately.

TECHNIQUE

When the polenta is cooled and firm, stamp out rounds, using a 4 cm (1½ inch) plain cutter.

ROASTED MIXED WINTER VEGETABLES

Root vegetables roasted together with olive oil make a wonderful partner to any winter meat or poultry dish. The sweet juices from the vegetables caramelise during cooking and give them a beautiful glaze and delicious flavour. Cardamoms add a hint of aroma, without being overpowering.

SERVES 6-8

350 g (12 oz) carrots
350 g (12 oz) parsnips
350 g (12 oz) celeriac
350 g (12 oz) sweet potato
150 ml (¼ pint) olive oil
4 cardamom pods, lightly
  crushed
15 ml (1 tbsp) soft brown
  sugar
coarse sea salt and pepper

PREPARATION TIME
20 minutes
COOKING TIME
About 1 hour
FREEZING
Not suitable

355-265 CALS PER SERVING

1. Preheat the oven to 200°C (400°F) Mark 6. Peel all of the vegetables. Quarter the carrots and parsnips lengthwise. Cut the celeriac and sweet potato into chunks.

2. Heat the olive oil in a roasting tin and add the vegetables, turning them to coat well. Roast in the oven for 30 minutes, turning the vegetables twice during cooking.

3. Add the crushed cardamom pods and the brown sugar to the vegetables, turning them to coat evenly. Return to the oven and bake for a further 30 minutes. The vegetables should look very browned and be completely soft, but not disintegrating.

4. Season liberally with coarse salt and pepper and transfer to a warmed serving dish to serve.

TECHNIQUE

Add the vegetables to the hot olive oil in the roasting tin and turn them to coat thoroughly with the oil.

VARIATION

For a more distinctive flavour, try replacing the brown sugar with maple syrup or honey. Toss in a handful of raisins 2 minutes before the end of the cooking time, too.

SHREDDED BRUSSELS SPROUTS WITH BACON

These buttery shredded sprouts are stir-fried with crispy cubes of bacon. They make an interesting change from traditional boiled or steamed Brussels sprouts and look so attractive. Use lightly smoked bacon, buying it in a piece if possible.

SERVES 4

700 g (1½ lb) Brussels
    sprouts
175 g (6 oz) piece smoked
    bacon
50 g (2 oz) butter
60 ml (4 tbsp) double cream
10 ml (2 tsp) caraway seeds
salt and pepper
freshly grated nutmeg

PREPARATION TIME
10 minutes
COOKING TIME
7 minutes
FREEZING
Not suitable

300 CALS PER SERVING

1. Trim the Brussels sprouts and shred them very finely. Remove the rind from the bacon, then cut into small cubes.

2. Heat a wok or frying pan and add the bacon. Cook over a high heat, stirring all the time, until the fat runs and the bacon is browning and crisp. Stir in the butter.

3. Toss in the Brussels sprouts and stir-fry over a high heat for 2-3 minutes until they begin to wilt. Pour in the cream, add the caraway seeds and stir-fry for 1 minute. Season with salt, pepper and nutmeg. Transfer to a warmed serving dish. Serve immediately.

NOTE: Cubed gammon would be good instead of bacon but you will need to fry it in a little butter rather than dry-fry.

VARIATION

Replace the Brussels sprouts with Savoy cabbage, or white cabbage.

TECHNIQUE

Cut the Brussels sprouts into fine shreds, using a sharp knife.

CLEMENTINE, CHICORY AND PEANUT SALAD

A crisp and colourful winter salad, combining juicy clementines, crunchy chicory, tangy spring onions and peppery radishes, tossed in a spicy peanut dressing. This salad brings a taste of summer to the depths of winter and is perfect served as a contrast to rich festive buffet food. It can also be prepared in advance.

SERVES 4

4 clementines

4 spring onions

2 heads of chicory

6 radishes

125 g (4 oz) natural peanuts

30 ml (2 tbsp) snipped fresh chives

PEANUT DRESSING

30 ml (2 tbsp) peanut butter

60 ml (4 tbsp) sunflower oil

30 ml (2 tbsp) white wine

15 ml (1 tbsp) white wine vinegar

15 ml (1 tbsp) light soy sauce

PREPARATION TIME
20 minutes
COOKING TIME
Nil
FREEZING
Not suitable

395 CALS PER SERVING

1. Peel the clementines and carefully remove any white membrane still clinging to them. Divide into segments and check that no white membrane remains. Place in a salad bowl.

2. Trim and slice the spring onions and add them to the bowl. Cut out the core of the chicory heads and shred the leaves, adding them to the bowl. Trim and quarter the radishes and add them to the bowl.

3. To make the dressing, place all the ingredients in a screw-topped jar and shake vigorously until well combined.

4. Pour the dressing over the salad and toss to mix. Scatter over the peanuts and chives. Serve immediately.

NOTE: If making the salad in advance, prepare all the vegetables and fruit. Store in plastic bags in the refrigerator until ready to serve, then toss in the dressing.

VARIATION

Replace the chicory with ½ red cabbage, very finely shredded; replace the chives with 30 ml (2 tbsp) sultanas.

TECHNIQUE

Peel the clementines and make sure that you remove any white membrane still clinging to them.

BEETROOT, CUCUMBER AND SPRING ONION SALAD

This sweet and sour salad – with its creamy dill dressing – is quick to make and has a delicious earthy flavour. You can buy ready-cooked beetroot for convenience, but cooking your own is well worth the effort. Cooked beetroot keeps well in the refrigerator and is a good base for salads and hot dishes.

SERVES 6

700 g (1½ lb) cooked
   beetroot
1 medium cucumber
4 pickled dill cucumbers
6 spring onions
DRESSING
150 ml (¼ pint) sunflower
   oil
1 egg
45 ml (3 tbsp) Dijon
   mustard
30 ml (2 tbsp) chopped fresh
   dill
5 ml (1 tsp) raspberry or red
   wine vinegar
squeeze of lemon juice
salt and pepper
200 ml (7 fl oz) soured
   cream or crème fraîche
TO GARNISH
dill sprigs

PREPARATION TIME
25 minutes
COOKING TIME
Nil
FREEZING
Not suitable

360 CALS PER SERVING

1. Peel the beetroot and cut into sticks. Halve the cucumber and cut into sticks – the same size as the beetroot. Dice the dill cucumbers. Trim and slice the spring onions.

2. Arrange the beetroot on a flat plate, or in a shallow dish. Arrange the cucumber over the beetroot. Scatter the diced dill cucumber and spring onions on top.

3. To make the dressing, place 45 ml (3 tbsp) sunflower oil in a blender or food processor and add the egg, mustard, dill, wine vinegar, lemon juice, and salt and pepper. Blend for a few seconds until evenly mixed and thickened. With the machine running, pour in the rest of the oil in a thin steady stream. Stir in the soured cream or crème fraîche.

4. Drizzle the dressing over the salad and garnish with dill sprigs to serve.

NOTE: The earthy flavour of freshly cooked beetroot complements the cucumber and is sharpened by the pickled dill cucumber. Pickled beetroot is not suitable, because it would mask the delicate flavours.

TECHNIQUE

Cut the cucumber into matchstick strips, the same size as the beetroot.

CHRISTMAS PUDDING

A rich and sticky figgy pudding packed with dried fruits plumped up with brandy and porter. The pudding is kept moist with butter instead of suet and is lightened with fresh breadcrumbs. It can be steamed in any heatproof bowl or mould – old jelly moulds make lovely shapes.

MAKES 2 PUDDINGS
EACH SERVES 8-10

two 225 g (8 oz) packets
   dried mixed fruit salad
125 g (4 oz) dried dates
225 g (8 oz) sultanas
225 g (8 oz) seedless raisins
150 ml (¼ pint) porter
60 ml (4 tbsp) brandy, dark
   rum or armagnac
1 lemon
1 orange
125 g (4 oz) ready-to-eat figs
125 g (4 oz) preserved stem
   or crystallised ginger
225 g (8 oz) whole
   unblanched almonds
225 g (8 oz) fresh brown
   breadcrumbs
225 g (8 oz) dark
   muscovado sugar
5 ml (1 tsp) grated nutmeg
5 ml (1 tsp) ground cinnamon
5 ml (1 tsp) ground ginger
175 g (6 oz) butter, chilled
4 eggs (size 2)
TO SERVE
90 ml (6 tbsp) brandy

PREPARATION TIME
30 minutes, plus overnight soaking
COOKING TIME
6 hours, plus 2 hours reheating
FREEZING
Suitable: Stage 5

465-370 CALS PER SERVING

1. Place the dried fruit salad, dried dates, sultanas and raisins in a shallow bowl and pour over the porter or stout and brandy. Grate the rind from the lemon and orange and reserve; squeeze the juice and add to the dried fruits. Stir well, cover and leave to soak overnight, stirring occasionally.

2. The next day, drain the soaked fruit, reserving any juices; discard any stones. Roughly chop the fruit, figs and ginger; place in a large mixing bowl.

3. Stir in the almonds, breadcrumbs, sugar and spices. Grate the butter and fold into the mixture. Beat the eggs with any liquid remaining from the soaked fruit and stir into the mixture with the reserved orange and lemon rind.

4. Butter two 1.2 litre (2 pint) pudding basins (or decorative metal or porcelain jelly moulds). Divide the mixture equally between the two, smoothing the surface. Cover with pleated double greaseproof paper (this allows the pudding to expand whilst cooking), and top with a pleated sheet of foil. Secure with string and make a handle to help lift the puddings out of the pan(s).

5. Place the puddings in one or two large saucepans and pour in enough boiling water to come halfway up the sides of the basins. Cover and steam for 6 hours, checking the water level and topping up

with *boiling* water as necessary. *Do not let the pans boil dry.* Cool completely, then wrap in fresh greaseproof paper and foil and store in a cool place until needed.

6. To serve, steam each pudding as before for 2 hours. Remove the papers and turn out onto a warmed serving dish. Heat the brandy in a small pan and pour over the pudding. Ignite with a match or taper and tip the plate from time to time to burn off all the alcohol. Serve with brandy or rum butter, or a thin real custard.

NOTE: If porter is unobtainable, use sweet stout instead.

TECHNIQUE

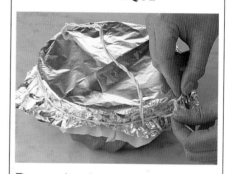

Tie securely with a piece of string and make a handle to help lift the pudding out of the pan once it is cooked.

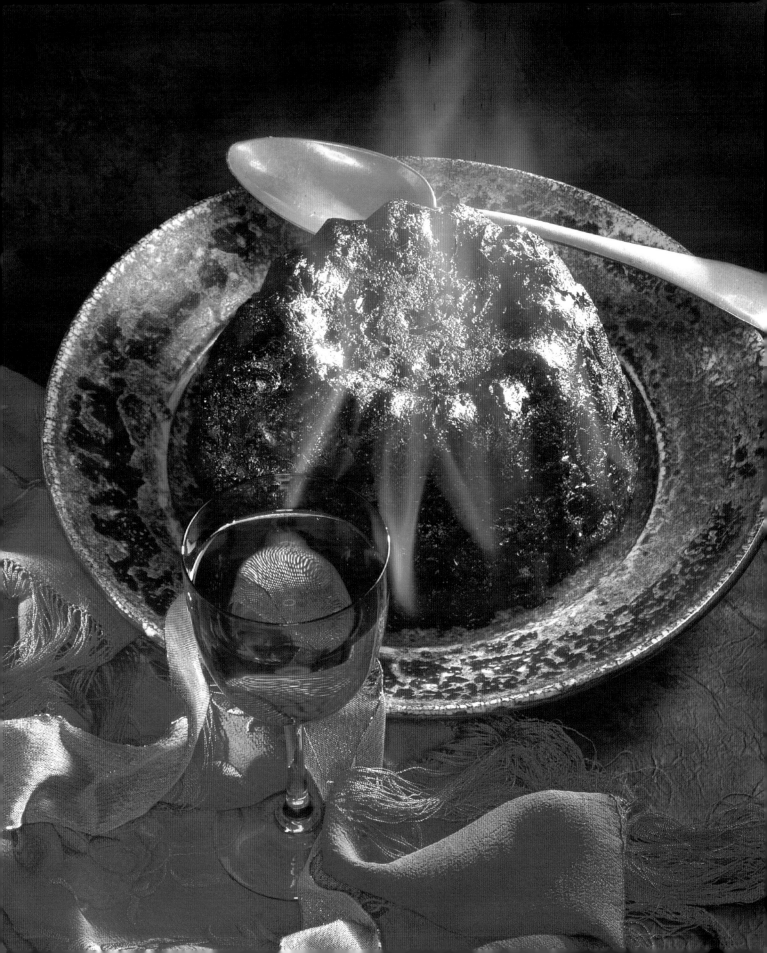

MINCEMEAT FLAN

A rich crumbly orange and almond pastry case is filled with homemade mincemeat and banana, then topped with a border of honey-glazed grilled star fruit. The mincemeat needs to be prepared at least 2 weeks ahead to allow time to mature. Alternatively you could buy some 'luxury mincemeat' instead.

SERVES 10

MINCEMEAT

1 large cooking apple
50 g (2 oz) glacé cherries
50 g (2 oz) blanched almonds
225 g (8 oz) currants
225 g (8 oz) sultanas
125 g (4 oz) chopped peel
225 g (8 oz) soft dark brown
  sugar
125 g (4 oz) shredded suet
5 ml (1 tsp) ground cinnamon
2.5 ml (½ tsp) grated nutmeg
grated rind and juice of
  1 orange
150 ml (¼ pint) brandy or rum

PASTRY

50 g (2 oz) blanched almonds
125 g (4 oz) plain white flour
grated rind and juice of
  1 orange
50 g (2 oz) caster sugar
50 g (2 oz) butter, cubed
1 egg yolk

TO ASSEMBLE

3 medium bananas
lemon juice, for sprinkling
3 ripe medium star fruit
thin honey, for brushing

PREPARATION TIME
40 minutes, plus standing
COOKING TIME
35-40 minutes
FREEZING
Suitable: Before baking

415 CALS PER SERVING

1. To make the mincemeat, core and grate the apple; roughly chop the cherries and nuts. Place in a large bowl. Work the currants and sultanas in a food processor for 30 seconds, just to break them up, then stir into the apple mixture, together with all the remaining ingredients. Mix well. Cover and leave to macerate for 2 days in a cool place. Pack into sterilised jars and seal.

2. For the pastry, toast the almonds until evenly golden; do not let burn. Allow to cool *completely*, then grind finely in a food processor or electric grinder.

3. Sift the flour and pinch of salt into a bowl and stir in the almonds, orange rind and sugar. Rub in the butter until mixture resembles fine breadcrumbs. Beat the egg yolk with 30 ml (2 tbsp) orange juice and stir into the pastry until it begins to hold together; add more juice if necessary to bind the pastry. Gather the dough into a ball and knead lightly on a clean work surface until smooth. Wrap and chill for at least 1 hour. (The pastry is quite fragile and crumbly).

4. Allow the pastry to come to room temperature. Peel the bananas, cut into cubes and toss in lemon juice. Mix with two thirds of the mincemeat; set aside.

5. Roll out the pastry and use to line a 2.5 cm (1 inch) deep, 23 cm (9 inch) fluted flan tin. Chill for 15 minutes.

6. Preheat the oven to 190°C (375°F) Mark 5. Spoon the mincemeat and banana mixture evenly into the flan. Bake for 35-40 minutes until the pastry is golden brown.

7. Meanwhile, preheat the grill to high. Cut the star fruit into 5 mm (¼ inch) slices and place on a foil-lined grill pan. Brush with a little warmed honey and brown under the grill for 3-5 minutes; watch them closely! Allow to cool.

8. Decorate the flan with the star fruit and serve warm.

NOTE: The basic mincemeat recipe makes about 1.4 kg (3 lb), which is more than you will need for this flan. Use the rest to make individual festive mince pies.

TECHNIQUE

Lift the pastry into the flan tin and press well into the fluted edge. If it breaks, simply patch it up – imperfections won't show!

LYCHEE AND COCONUT SYLLABUB

Syllabubs were originally served to cleanse and sharpen the palate, but this one is somewhat richer! A delicious soft coconut cream conceals a layer of luscious lychees. Canned ones will do at a pinch, if fresh are not available. Alternatively pineapple and rambutans make good alternatives.

SERVES 6

75 g (3 oz) creamed coconut
150 ml (¼ pint) sweet
  dessert wine, such as
  Moscatel de Valencia
45 ml (3 tbsp) stem ginger
  syrup (see below)
24 fresh or canned lychees
75 ml (5 tbsp) coconut
  liqueur, such as Malibu
30 ml (2 tbsp) preserved
  stem ginger in syrup,
  drained
450 ml (¾ pint) double
  cream
TO DECORATE
coconut shreds

PREPARATION TIME
30 minutes, plus chilling
COOKING TIME
Nil
FREEZING
Not suitable

450 CALS PER SERVING

1. Grate the coconut and place in saucepan with the sweet wine and ginger syrup. Heat very gently until the coconut is melted; *do not boil.* Stir well and leave to cool.

2. Peel the lychees, cut in half and remove the stones. Place in a bowl and pour over the coconut liqueur. Chop the stem ginger, and stir into the lychee mixture. Cover and chill for at least 30 minutes.

3. Whisk the cream until it holds soft peaks. Gently fold in the coconut and wine mixture. The mixture should hold its shape – if it is a little runny, whisk lightly until it thickens.

4. Divide the lychees and liqueur between 6 tall glasses. Spoon over the coconut cream syllabub, then chill for at least 30 minutes before serving.

5. For the decoration, toast some of the coconut shreds. Arrange the plain and toasted coconut shreds on the syllabubs to serve.

NOTE: Don't be tempted to use coconut milk or instant coconut milk for this – it will not taste the same.

VARIATION

Omit the ginger and ginger syrup. Replace with the grated rind of 1 lemon or lime and 45 ml (3 tbsp) sugar syrup.

TECHNIQUE

Peel the lychees, then halve to remove the stones.

PINEAPPLE AND DATE SALAD WITH KUMQUATS

An ideal dessert to follow a rich festive dinner, this pretty fruit salad is made with seasonal oranges, kumquats, pineapple, fresh or dried dates and a sprinkling of walnuts. The kumquats are poached in an acacia honey syrup and acquire a wonderful musky flavour.

SERVES 6

75 ml (5 tbsp) acacia honey
50 g (2 oz) soft brown sugar
300 ml (½ pint) Earl Grey
   tea, strained
225 g (8 oz) kumquats
2 oranges
I medium pineapple
12 fresh or dried dates
125 g (4 oz) walnut halves

PREPARATION TIME
35 minutes, plus chilling
COOKING TIME
15 minutes
FREEZING
Not suitable

330 CALS PER SERVING

I. First make the syrup. Place the honey, sugar and tea in a saucepan and bring to the boil. Boil for I minute. Halve the kumquats horizontally and place in the syrup. Simmer uncovered for about 10 minutes until the kumquats are tender. Leave to cool in the syrup.

2. Peel the oranges as you would an apple, removing all the rind and white pith. Slice them crosswise and place in a bowl. Using a sharp knife, cut the top and bottom off the pineapple and cut away the skin. Cut out the brown 'eyes'. Quarter the pineapple lengthways and cut out the core. Cut the flesh into large chunks. Carefully mix with the oranges.

3. Halve the dates and remove the stones. Stir into the fruit mixture with the walnuts. Drain the kumquats and set aside; strain the syrup and pour over the fruit in the bowl. Cover and chill for I hour.

4. Spoon the fruit salad into a serving dish or individual glass bowls and scatter the kumquats on top. Serve with whipped cream.

NOTE: Kumquats are readily available at Christmas and have a sharp perfumed flavour. Some stores sell crystallised kumquats which are ideal for decorating desserts and cakes.

VARIATION

Substitute 4 ripe pears for the pineapple and cook the kumquats in a syrup flavoured with jasmine tea rather than Earl Grey.

TECHNIQUE

Peel the oranges with a sharp knife, taking care to remove all the white pith.

RASPBERRY AND ALMOND TRIFLE

An unusual trifle of ratafias and toasted almonds soaked in almond liqueur, covered with fresh or frozen raspberries, then topped with a rich syllabub flavoured with Madeira and almond liqueur. For a less alcoholic version, omit sprinkling the ratafias with liqueur.

SERVES 6

125 g (4 oz) blanched almonds

450 g (1 lb) fresh or frozen raspberries

finely grated rind and juice of 1 lemon

icing sugar, to taste

225 g (8 oz) ratafias (see note)

75 ml (5 tbsp) Amaretto di Saronno, or other almond liqueur

150 ml (¼ pint) dry Madeira or sherry

freshly grated nutmeg

450 ml (¾ pint) double cream

TO DECORATE

gold and silver sugared almonds

silver balls (optional)

extra ratafias

PREPARATION TIME
30 minutes, plus chilling
COOKING TIME
Nil
FREEZING
Not suitable

725 CALS PER SERVING

1. Place the almonds on a tray and toast under the grill or in a moderate oven until evenly golden. Allow to cool, then chop roughly.

2. Purée half of the raspberries in a blender or food processor. Sieve to remove the pips and stir in the lemon juice and icing sugar to taste.

3. Divide the ratafias between individual serving glasses and sprinkle with the toasted almonds and 45 ml (3 tbsp) almond liqueur. Scatter over the whole raspberries and sprinkle with a little icing sugar. Pour over the raspberry purée. Cover and chill in the refrigerator.

4. Meanwhile, put the lemon rind in a bowl with the Madeira or sherry, remaining liqueur and nutmeg. Leave to macerate for at least 1 hour, then strain.

5. Whisk the cream with icing sugar to taste until just beginning to thicken, then gradually whisk in the flavoured wine and liqueur until the mixture holds soft peaks. Spoon over the raspberries and ratafias. Cover and chill for at least 1 hour before serving.

6. Just before serving, decorate with gold and silver sugared almonds, silver balls if using, and extra ratafias.

NOTE: Ratafias are tiny crunchy almond biscuits. If unobtainable, use amaretti or macaroons instead. If preferred, assemble the trifle in a large serving dish.

VARIATION

Substitute fresh or frozen blackberries for the raspberries and use crème de cassis instead of almond liqueur.

TECHNIQUE

Sieve the puréed raspberries, using a nylon sieve and pressing the pulp through with the back of a spoon.

CHESTNUT MERINGUE ICE WITH ORANGE CARAMEL SAUCE

A no-need-to-stir luxurious ice cream, comprising crushed cinnamon meringue, chopped marrons glacés, liqueur-laced cream and chestnut purée. An orange, caramel and liqueur sauce is the perfect complement. The alcohol in the ice cream stops it becoming too solid, so you can serve it straight from the freezer.

SERVES 8

4 egg whites
225 g (8 oz) caster sugar
5 ml (1 tsp) ground
    cinnamon
8 marrons glacés
500 g (1 lb 2 oz) can
    sweetened chestnut purée
about 45 ml (3 tbsp) Kahlua,
    Tia Maria or other coffee
    or chocolate liqueur
300 ml (½ pint) double
    cream
**ORANGE CARAMEL
SAUCE**
2 oranges
about 450 ml (¾ pint)
    freshly squeezed orange
    juice
225 g (8 oz) granulated
    sugar
30 ml (2 tbsp) Grand
    Marnier or other orange-
    flavoured liqueur

PREPARATION TIME
25 minutes, plus freezing
COOKING TIME
2½-3 hours
FREEZING
Suitable: For up to 1 week

580 CALS PER SERVING

1. Preheat the oven to 110°C (225°F) Mark ¼. Line a large baking sheet with non-stick baking parchment. Whisk the egg whites in a large bowl until stiff but not dry. Whisk in the sugar a spoonful at a time, whisking until very stiff between each addition. Whisk in the cinnamon. Spoon into mounds on the lined baking sheet. Bake in the oven for 2½-3 hours. Lift the meringues off the paper and transfer to a wire rack to cool.

2. To make the sauce, finely pare the rind from the oranges and cut into very fine shreds. Squeeze the juice and strain into a measuring jug; make up to 600 ml (1 pint) with more orange juice.

3. Place the sugar in a saucepan with 45 ml (3 tbsp) water and dissolve over a gentle heat without stirring. Once dissolved, bring to the boil and boil rapidly until the sugar turns a rich golden brown. Immediately pour in the orange juice, taking great care as it will splutter. Stir over a gentle heat until the caramel dissolves, add the orange rind shreds and boil rapidly to reduce to a thin syrup. Let cool, then stir in the liqueur. Set aside.

4. Line a 900 g (2 lb) loaf tin with cling film. Roughly chop the marrons glacés. In a large bowl, beat the chestnut purée

with the liqueur. In another bowl, whisk the cream until it just holds its shape, then fold into the chestnut purée.

5. Lightly crush the meringues, then fold into the cream mixture with the chopped chestnuts. Spoon into the prepared loaf tin, packing the mixture down well. Level the surface, cover and freeze for at least 4 hours or until firm.

6. To serve, turn the ice cream out onto a board, remove cling film and cut into slices, using a hot knife. Serve with the warm or cold orange caramel sauce.

NOTE: Marrons glacés are crystallised sweet chestnuts which are readily available at Christmas. If serving the sauce cold, thin it with a little extra orange juice.

TECHNIQUE

Place the meringues in a plastic bag and crush lightly with the heel of your hand.

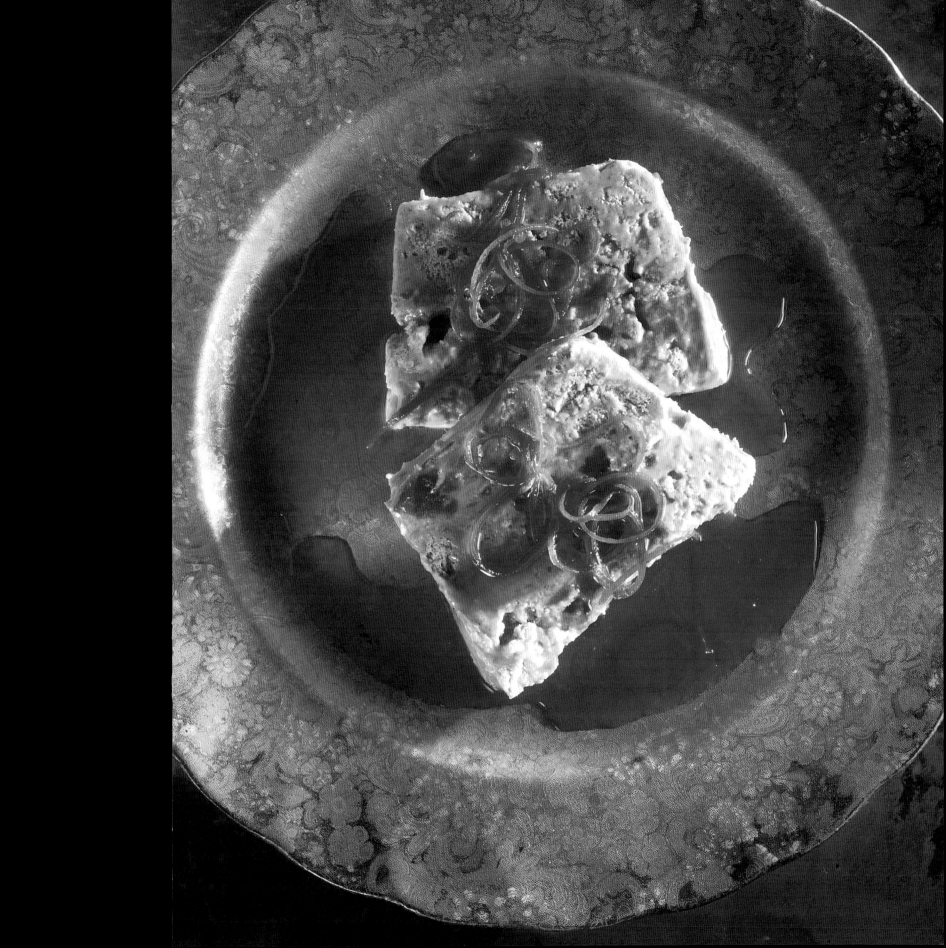

BOTTLED SPICED PEARS, PEACHES AND NECTARINES

Beautiful bottled fruits – picked when in their prime and poached in a sweet-sour and spiced sugar syrup – make lovely Christmas gifts. They are particularly delicious served with hot or cold ham. Use whole spices for optimum flavour and effect.

MAKES 900 G (2 LB)

900 g (2 lb) ripe but firm
  unblemished William
  pears
2.5 cm (1 inch) piece fresh
  root ginger
1 lemon
450 g (1 lb) golden
  granulated sugar
300 ml (½ pint) white wine
  vinegar
300 ml (½ pint) clear malt
  vinegar
15 ml (1 tbsp) allspice
  berries
15 ml (1 tbsp) cloves
1 large cinnamon stick or
  several pieces of cassia
  bark

PREPARATION TIME
20 minutes
COOKING TIME
About 20 minutes
FREEZING
Not suitable

55 CALS PER SERVING

1. Carefully peel the pears. Halve or quarter them, then remove the cores. Place in a bowl of water with a little vinegar added to prevent discolouration.

2. Thinly slice the ginger and pare the rind off the lemon in a single strip. Put the sugar and vinegars into a saucepan and dissolve over a gentle heat. When dissolved, add the ginger, lemon rind, spices and drained pears. Slowly bring to the boil and simmer gently for about 20 minutes or until the pears are just tender – they must remain whole.

3. Lift out the pears with a slotted spoon and pack into sterilised jars, with an even distribution of the cooked spices.

4. Bring the syrup to the boil and boil for 10 minutes or until syrupy. Pour over the pears, making sure they are all covered. Seal and store in a cool dark place for up to 6 months.

NOTE: Do not use over-ripe fruit or it will discolour and disintegrate during cooking.

VARIATIONS

For spiced peaches or nectarines, prepare in exactly the same manner, but skin, halve and remove the stones from the fruit. Use orange instead of lemon rind and omit the ginger.

TECHNIQUE

Add the pear quarters to the vinegar syrup with the ginger, spices and lemon rind.

CRANBERRY AND ROAST SHALLOT CHUTNEY

A dark ruby-red relish made with sharp flavourful cranberries and chunks of sweet caramelised shallots simmered together with a dash of crème de cassis. Unlike the usual cranberry sauce, this is more versatile and a little sharper, which makes it a perfect accompaniment to farmhouse cheese, thick slices of cold ham and, of course, the cold Christmas turkey!

MAKES 900 G (2 LB)

450 g (1 lb) shallots
45 ml (3 tbsp) olive oil
225 g (8 oz) soft brown
    sugar
salt and pepper
450 g (1 lb) fresh or frozen
    cranberries
2.5 cm (1 inch) piece fresh
    root ginger
15 ml (1 tbsp) mustard
    seeds
150 ml ($\frac{1}{4}$ pint) red wine
200 ml (7 fl oz) red wine
    vinegar
45 ml (3 tbsp) crème de
    cassis liqueur

PREPARATION TIME
25 minutes
COOKING TIME
About 30 minutes
FREEZING
Not suitable

45 CALS PER 25 G (1 OZ)

1. Preheat the oven to 200°C (400°F) Mark 6. Plunge the shallots into a pan of boiling water for 5 minutes to loosen the skins, then remove. When cool enough to handle, carefully peel, leaving on a little root end to hold them intact.

2. Halve the shallots lengthwise and place in a roasting tin with the olive oil and 45 ml (3 tbsp) of the sugar. Roast in the oven for at least 30 minutes, turning twice until softened and caramelised, but not burnt. Season generously with salt and pepper.

3. Meanwhile, pick over the cranberries, discarding any discoloured ones. Peel and finely grate the ginger root. Place the cranberries in a heavy-based saucepan with the ginger, remaining sugar, mustard seeds, red wine and vinegar. Bring slowly to the boil and simmer for 10-15 minutes until the cranberries burst and the mixture thickens. Remove from the heat.

4. Stir the shallots into the softened cranberries. Deglaze the roasting tin with the liqueur and reduce until syrupy, then pour into the cranberry mixture. Return to the heat and simmer very gently, stirring occasionally, for 10-15 minutes or until the chutney is thick.

5. Spoon the chutney into warm sterilised jars. Seal and store in a cool dry place for up to 6 months. Alternatively store in a plastic container in the refrigerator for up to 1 month. Serve with cheese, or hot or cold meats – particularly ham, turkey and game.

TECHNIQUE

Turn the shallots during roasting, taking care not to break them up too much.

PUMPKIN, APRICOT AND ALMOND CHUTNEY

A sunny golden chutney to serve with cold meats and cheese, or to offer as a Christmas gift. It must be allowed to mature and mellow for at least 1 month before using. Pumpkin and apricots go very well together – you will find most greengrocers sell pumpkin by the wedge during autumn and winter.

MAKES 1.8 KG (4 LB)

450 g (1 lb) wedge of
   pumpkin
2 large onions
225 g (8 oz) dried apricots
   (not no-need-to-soak)
600 ml (1 pint) cider vinegar
450 g (1 lb) soft light brown
   sugar
225 g (8 oz) sultanas
finely grated rind and juice
   of 1 orange
30 ml (2 tbsp) salt
2.5 ml ($\frac{1}{2}$ tsp) turmeric
2 cardamom pods, crushed
5 ml (1 tsp) mild chilli
   seasoning
10 ml (2 tsp) coriander
   seeds
125 g (4 oz) blanched
   almonds

PREPARATION TIME
30 minutes
COOKING TIME
$\frac{3}{4}$-1$\frac{1}{4}$ hours
FREEZING
Not suitable

50 CALS PER 25 G (1 OZ)

1. Remove any seeds from the pumpkin and cut off the skin. Cut the flesh into 2.5 cm (1 inch) cubes. Peel and slice the onions. Cut the dried apricots into chunks.

2. Place the vinegar and sugar in a large heavy-based saucepan and bring to the boil. Add the pumpkin, dried apricots and onions, together with all the remaining ingredients, except the almonds. Stir well and bring to the boil.

3. Turn down the heat and cook gently until soft and thick, stirring occasionally whilst runny, but more frequently as the chutney thickens. *Do not let it catch and burn.* The mixture may take between 45 minutes and 1$\frac{1}{4}$ hours to thicken and cook; don't let it become too dry. To test, draw a wooden spoon through the mixture – it should leave a clear trail at the bottom of the pan which fills up slowly.

4. Stir in the almonds and pack the chutney into warm sterilised jars (it won't matter if they are still wet). Seal and store in a cool dark place for at least 1 month before using. Serve with cheese and cold meats.

NOTE: Use a heavy aluminium pan or a stainless steel pan, not an unlined copper pan which would taint the chutney. Never leave chutney whilst it is cooking as it can easily burn towards the end.

PRUNE AND APPLE CHUTNEY

Use 450 g (1 lb) cooking apples and 225 g (8 oz) stoned prunes in place of the pumpkin and apricots. Substitute lemon, raisins and walnuts for the orange, sultanas and almonds. Instead of the spices listed, use 10 ml (2 tsp) mustard seeds, 1 cinnamon stick and 3 cloves.

TECHNIQUE

To check whether the chutney is ready, draw a wooden spoon through the mixture. It should leave a clear trail on the bottom of the pan which fills up slowly.

SCOTS TABLET

This is a delectable sweet which simply melts in the mouth and is quite addictive. Arranged in small boxes or jars it makes an ideal gift. It is a little like fudge, but much crisper, and not at all chewy. Tablet is quite straight-forward to make as long as you follow the instructions carefully. As the temperature is crucial to the texture, a sugar thermometer is necessary – unless you are totally confident about testing for the hard-ball stage.

MAKES 450 G (1 LB)

450 g (1 lb) granulated sugar
150 ml (¼ pint) evaporated milk
pinch of salt
2.5 ml (½ tsp) vanilla essence

PREPARATION TIME
10 minutes
COOKING TIME
About 20 minutes
FREEZING
Not suitable

85 CALS PER 25 G (1 OZ)

1. Butter a 20 cm (8 inch) shallow square cake tin. Fill a shallow roasting tin with cold water.

2. Place the sugar in a heavy-based medium saucepan with the evaporated milk. Heat *very* gently, stirring occasionally, until the sugar is *completely* dissolved. Do not let the mixture boil during this time or it will crystallise. Do not use a non-stick pan or it will burn.

3. Once completely dissolved, bring to the boil and boil for about 20 minutes or until it registers 118°C (245°F) on a sugar thermometer (ie the hard ball stage – when a little of the mixture will form a hard ball when rolled between your fingers). Immediately stand the base of the pan in the cold water and stir in the salt and vanilla essence.

4. Remove the pan from the water and beat the mixture as it begins to 'set' and go grainy around the edge of the pan, pulling this crust towards the centre. Do not overbeat, otherwise the mixture will not pour; if underbeaten, the tablet will be chewy – which is all wrong!

5. While still pourable, pour the mixture into the prepared tin and allow to cool slightly until set. Mark into squares or bars and leave until completely cold, then cut or break into squares or bars. Store in an airtight container.

NOTE: It may take a couple of attempts to perfect tablet, but it is worth the effort. It should be hard to the touch, and granular and melting in the mouth.

VARIATIONS

● Stir 45 ml (3 tbsp) dessicated coconut into the syrup at stage 3 before beating.
● Stir 30 ml (2 tbsp) chopped crystallised ginger into the mixture after beating.
● Stir 125 g (4 oz) chocolate drops into the mixture after beating.

TECHNIQUE

Beat the mixture as it begins to go grainy and 'set' around the edge of the pan, drawing this crust into the centre.

CHOCOLATE TRUFFLES

These luscious liqueur-laced bitter chocolate truffles make very acceptable gifts. They are either covered with a chocolate coating, or simply rolled in cocoa powder, chopped nuts, coconut or grated chocolate. As the texture is a little soft at room temperature rolled truffles, in particular, should be stored in the refrigerator.

MAKES ABOUT 24

BASIC MIXTURE
225 g (8 oz) quality bitter, plain or milk chocolate
90 ml (3 fl oz) double cream
45 ml (3 tbsp) brandy, rum, orange liqueur, coffee liqueur, coconut liqueur, or vanilla essence

UNDIPPED TRUFFLES
cocoa powder, chopped nuts, dessicated or grated coconut, chocolate vermicelli or grated chocolate, for rolling

DIPPED TRUFFLES
350 g (12 oz) quality plain, milk or white chocolate (or a combination of all three), in small pieces

PREPARATION TIME
30 minutes-1 hour, plus chilling (and overnight freezing for dipped truffles)
COOKING TIME
Nil
FREEZING
Suitable: Open freeze, then pack in a box. Thaw in refrigerator.

65 CALS PER TRUFFLE

1. To prepare the basic truffle mixture, grate the chocolate into a small bowl and add the cream. Stand the bowl over a pan of simmering water. Heat very gently until the chocolate begins to melt. Stir well until smooth and remove from the heat. Leave to cool for about 20-30 minutes to room temperature; the mixture should have thickened considerably.

2. Beat in the brandy, rum, liqueur or vanilla. Using an electric whisk, beat for about 5 minutes until the mixture is light, fluffy and paler in colour. It should be firm enough to stand in peaks. Spoon into a shallow tin, cover and refrigerate for at least 2 hours until quite firm.

3. To make simple rolled truffles, sprinkle a tray with cocoa powder and place even-sized teaspoonfuls of truffle mixture on the tray. Dust your hands with a little cocoa powder and quickly roll the mixture into uneven balls. If preferred roll the truffles in chopped nuts, coconut, chocolate vermicelli or grated chocolate. Place on waxed paper and refrigerate for at least 2 hours.

4. To make dipped truffles, roll the truffle mixture into neat 2.5 cm (1 inch) balls and place on a tray lined with waxed paper. Freeze overnight until rock hard.

5. Melt the chocolate for dipping over simmering water. Check the temperature with a sugar thermometer if possible: it should be 46-49°C (115°-120°F), or 43°C (110°F) for white chocolate.

6. Remove a few truffles at a time from the freezer. Spear each one with a cocktail stick and dip quickly into the chocolate. Shake off excess and place on a tray lined with non-stick baking parchment. Place in refrigerator for at least 2 hours to set. Repeat with remaining truffles.

7. Place the truffles in paper cases and pack in boxes. Store in the refrigerator for up to 10 days.

VARIATIONS

Pipe a contrasting colour of chocolate over the dipped truffles or apply a little edible gold leaf, to decorate. Alternatively, press a toasted flaked nut, sliver of crystallised ginger, or a quartered cherry onto the setting chocolate.

TECHNIQUE

Dip each truffle into the chocolate, turning to coat evenly.

LUXURY CHRISTMAS CAKE

Make this Christmas cake any time from mid-November to mid-December. Don't be tempted to use margarine – the butter gives a wonderful flavour and improves the cake's keeping qualities. Store tightly wrapped to prevent the cake from drying out; spear occasionally with a skewer and 'feed' with brandy.

MAKES 30-40 SLICES

1 lemon
1 orange
225 g (8 oz) dried apricots
175 g (6 oz) stoned prunes
175 g (6 oz) unblanched
   almonds
175 g (6 oz) glacé cherries
225 g (8 oz) currants
125 g (4 oz) sultanas
225 g (8 oz) raisins
150 ml (¼ pint) brandy, rum,
   porter or sweet stout
125 g (4 oz) chopped
   candied peel
350 g (12 oz) self-raising
   white flour
10 ml (2 tsp) mixed spice
300 g (10 oz) unsalted
   butter, softened
300 g (10 oz) soft dark
   muscovado sugar
6 (size 3) eggs, beaten
60 ml (4 tbsp) treacle
TO DECORATE
apricot glaze (see right)
450 g (1 lb) almond paste
450 g (1 lb) ready-to-roll
   fondant icing

PREPARATION TIME
1 hour, plus macerating
COOKING TIME
3-4 hours
FREEZING
Suitable: Stage 5

315-235 CALS PER SLICE

1. Grate the rind from the lemon and orange and squeeze the juice. Roughly chop the apricots, prunes and almonds. Wash, dry and halve the cherries. Mix the apricots, prunes and citrus rinds and juices together in a large bowl, with the currants, sultanas and raisins. Add the brandy (or other liquor), cover and leave to macerate overnight, stirring occasionally.

2. The next day, preheat the oven to 160°C (325°F) Mark 3. Line a 25 cm (10 inch) round or 23 cm (9 inch) square cake tin with a double or triple layer of greaseproof paper. Grease with butter.

3. Add the cherries, nuts and peel to the macerated fruit mixture and stir well. Sift the flour, spice and 2.5 ml (½ tsp) salt together. In a large bowl, cream together the butter and sugar until fluffy. Gradually beat in the eggs, beating well between each addition to prevent curdling. Stir in the treacle, then fold in the flour and fruit.

4. Spoon the mixture into the cake tin, level the surface, then make a slight hollow in the middle. Bake in the preheated oven for 1 hour, then reduce the temperature to 140°C (275°F) Mark 1 and bake for a further 2-3 hours. Cover the top of the cake with buttered paper if browning too much. Test by inserting a skewer into the centre of the cake – if it comes out clean, the cake is cooked.

5. Leave in the tin until cool enough to handle, then turn out onto a wire rack to cool completely in the paper. When cold, keep one layer of greaseproof paper on the cake, then wrap in foil. Store in a cool dry place.

6. Set the cake on a board. Up to 1 week before Christmas, brush the cake with apricot glaze and cover with almond paste (see page 5). Leave to dry for 24 hours, then cover with fondant icing and apply the decorations (see pages 6-7). Secure a ribbon around the cake if desired.

NOTE: Use seedless muscatel raisins if obtainable. Avoid using 'no-need-to soak' dried apricots and prunes.

APRICOT GLAZE: Gently heat 125 g (4 oz) apricot jam in a small pan with 30 ml (2 tbsp) water until melted. Boil for 1 minute, then sieve. Use warm.

TECHNIQUE

Line the cake tin with a double or triple layer of greaseproof paper.

CINNAMON CRANBERRY STREUSSEL CAKE

This streussel 'cake' most closely resembles a shortbread in texture and is delightful served, cut into wedges, with coffee. A layer of thick cranberry sauce in the middle provides a sharp contrast to the buttery cake.

SERVES 12

CRANBERRY SAUCE

225 g (8 oz) fresh or frozen
   cranberries

75 g (3 oz) caster sugar

juice of 1 orange

2.5 ml (½ tsp) ground mixed
   spice

STREUSSEL DOUGH

350 g (12 oz) butter

75 g (3 oz) caster sugar

45 ml (3 tbsp) olive oil

5 ml (1 tsp) vanilla essence

1 egg (size 2)

700 g (1½ lb) plain white
   flour

7.5 ml (1½ tsp) baking
   powder

2.5 ml (½ tsp) salt

15 ml (1 tbsp) ground
   cinnamon

TO DECORATE

icing sugar, for dredging

PREPARATION TIME
25 minutes, plus chilling
COOKING TIME
1¼-1½ hours
FREEZING
Not suitable

505 CALS PER SERVING

1. Place the cranberries in a food processor with the sugar and chop roughly. Transfer to a saucepan and add the orange juice and spice. Bring to the boil, stirring constantly. Lower the heat and simmer for 5 minutes, then set aside to cool completely.

2. To make the streussel dough, cream the butter and sugar together in a bowl until light and fluffy. Beat in the olive oil and vanilla essence. Lightly whisk the egg and beat into the mixture.

3. Sift the flour, baking powder, salt and cinnamon into a bowl. Gradually stir into the creamed mixture until the dough resembles a rough shortbread mixture. Bring the dough together with your hands and knead lightly into a ball. Wrap and chill in the refrigerator for at least 2 hours or until really firm.

4. Preheat the oven to 150°C (300°F) Mark 2. Line the base of a 25 cm (10 inch) spring-form cake tin with non-stick baking parchment. Grease and flour the sides of the tin.

5. Divide the well-chilled dough in half; rewrap one half and return to the refrigerator. Coarsely grate the other half into the tin to cover the bottom evenly.

6. Carefully spoon on the cranberry sauce, leaving 1 cm (½ inch) clear at the edge. Grate the remaining streussel dough evenly over the top. Bake in the oven for about 1¼-1½ hours until pale but firm. Dredge with icing sugar whilst still hot. Leave to cool in the tin, then loosen and carefully remove from the tin. Store in an airtight tin for up to 1 week. Serve cut into wedges.

VARIATION

Replace the cranberries with no-need-to-soak apricots and use the juice of 2 oranges. Proceed as above, but simmer until all the juice has evaporated and the apricots are soft. Stir in 50 g (2 oz) toasted flaked almonds.

Alternatively use 350 g (12 oz) mincemeat in place of the cranberry sauce.

TECHNIQUE

Coarsely grate the remaining streussel pastry over the top, to cover the filling completely.

CHRISTMAS MORNING MUFFINS

Moist muffins bursting with cranberries make a wonderful start to the celebrations! Have all the dry ingredients mixed together, and prepare the muffin tin the night before. On Christmas morning, just stir in the liquids and cranberries, fill the tins and bake. Serve from the oven – these muffins do not reheat well.

MAKES 12

175 g (6 oz) fresh
   cranberries
50 g (2 oz) icing sugar, sifted
150 g (5 oz) plain wholemeal
   flour
150 g (5 oz) plain white flour
15 ml (1 tbsp) baking
   powder
5 ml (1 tsp) ground mixed
   spice
2.5 ml (½ tsp) salt
50 g (2 oz) soft light brown
   sugar
1 egg
250 ml (8 fl oz) milk
60 ml (2 fl oz) vegetable oil

PREPARATION TIME
15 minutes
COOKING TIME
20 minutes
FREEZING
Not suitable

175 CALS PER MUFFIN

1. Halve the cranberries and place in a bowl with the icing sugar. Toss gently to mix.

2. Line a twelve-cup muffin tin with paper cases or simply grease with butter. Sift together the flours, baking powder, mixed spice, salt and soft brown sugar into a large bowl. Make a well in the centre.

3. Preheat the oven to 180°C (350°F) Mark 4. Beat the egg with the milk and oil. Add to the dry ingredients and stir just until blended, then lightly and quickly stir in the cranberries. The mixture should look roughly mixed, with lumps and floury pockets.

4. Two-thirds fill the muffin cups with the mixture. Bake in the oven for about 20 minutes or until well risen and golden brown.

5. Transfer the muffins to a wire rack to cool slightly. Serve whilst still warm, with crème fraîche if desired.

NOTE: If using a greased (rather than lined) muffin tin, on removing from the oven turn it upside down onto a wire rack and leave for 2 minutes to allow the steam to loosen the muffins. Lift off the tray and turn the muffins up the right way.

VARIATION

Substitute 225 g (8 oz) mincemeat for the cranberries. Add to the well in the middle of the dry ingredients with the liquid. Stir until just moistened but still lumpy. Fill the muffin tins and bake as above.

TECHNIQUE

Spoon the mixture into the paper cases, until each one is two-thirds full.

Shortbread

Shortbread is a traditional Scottish festive bake and no home north of the Border is complete without a home-made yuletide batch. With its rich buttery flavour, it really should melt in the mouth. A box or tin of shortbread also makes an ideal gift, especially if you include one or two of the variations suggested below.

MAKES 24-36

450 g (1 lb) butter
225 g (8 oz) caster sugar
450 g (1 lb) plain white flour
225 g (8 oz) ground rice or
    rice flour
pinch of salt
TO DECORATE
golden or coloured
    granulated sugar, for
    coating
caster sugar, for sprinkling

PREPARATION TIME
20 minutes, plus chilling
COOKING TIME
20 minutes
FREEZING
Not suitable

270 -180 CALS PER BISCUIT

1. Line 2 baking sheets with grease-proof paper. Make sure all the ingredients are at room temperature. Cream the butter and sugar together in a bowl until pale and fluffy. Sift the flour, rice flour and salt together and stir into the creamed mixture, using a wooden spoon, until it resembles breadcrumbs.

2. Gather the dough together with your hand and turn onto a clean work surface. Knead lightly until it forms a ball, then lightly roll into a sausage, about 5-7.5 cm (2-3 inches) thick. Wrap in cling film and chill until firm.

3. Preheat the oven to 190°C (375°F) Mark 5. Unwrap the roll and slice into discs, about 7-10 mm ($\frac{1}{3}$-$\frac{1}{2}$ inch) thick. Pour golden or coloured granulated sugar onto a plate and roll the edge of each disc in the sugar. Place the biscuits, cut side up, on the baking sheets.

4. Bake for about 15-25 minutes, depending on thickness, until very pale golden. Remove from the oven and sprinkle with caster sugar. Allow to cool on the baking sheet for 10 minutes, then transfer to a wire rack to cool.

NOTE: Never overwork shortbread or it will become tough. Take care to avoid overcooking too – shortbread should never really colour, just set and turn very pale.

VARIATION

Spiced Shortbread: Sift 15 ml (1 tbsp) ground mixed spice with the flours.
Ginger Shortbread: Sift 5 ml (1 tsp) ground ginger with the flours. Add 50 g (2 oz) chopped crystallised ginger to the dough.
Chocolate Chip Shortbread: Knead 50 g (2 oz) chocolate chips into the dough.
Lavender Shortbread: Add the flowers from 6 lavender heads to the dough. Roll out the dough very thinly and cut into rounds with a biscuit cutter. Bake for 15 minutes only.
Rosemary Shortbread: Add 10 ml (2 tsp) chopped fresh rosemary to the dough. Roll out thinly and bake as for Lavender Shortbread.

TECHNIQUE

Roll the edge of each shortbread disc in coloured or golden granulated sugar before baking.

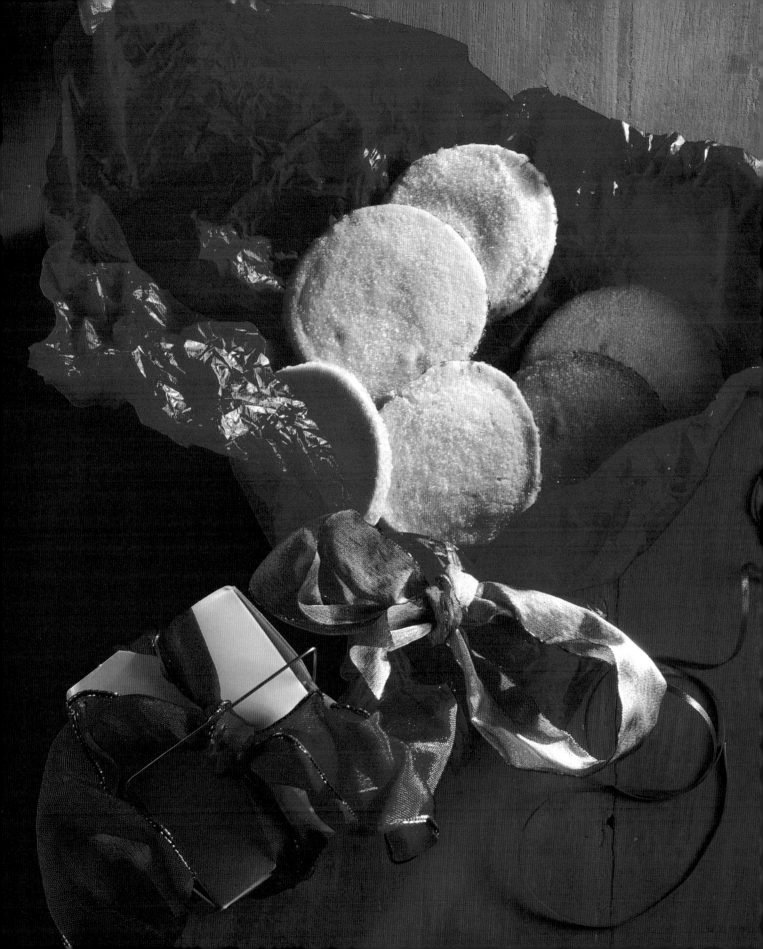

ALMOND CRESCENTS

These heavenly crisp pastry crescents conceal a deliciously moist ground almond filling. After baking they are sprinkled with orange flower water and rolled in icing sugar to give a thick outer crust. The orange flower water is very traditional in Morocco – their land of origin – and perfectly complements the almond flavour.

MAKES ABOUT 18

ALMOND PASTE
50 g (2 oz) butter
225 g (8 oz) ground almonds
2.5 ml ($\frac{1}{2}$ tsp) almond essence
45 ml (3 tbsp) icing sugar
45 ml (3 tbsp) orange flower water

PASTRY
225 g (8 oz) plain white flour
pinch of salt
15 g ($\frac{1}{2}$ oz) butter
45 ml (3 tbsp) orange flower water

TO DECORATE
orange flower water
icing sugar

PREPARATION TIME
45 minutes
COOKING TIME
15-20 minutes
FREEZING
Not suitable

160 CALS PER PASTRY

1. For the almond paste, melt the butter and allow to cool. Place the ground almonds, almond essence, icing sugar and orange flower water in a bowl. Mix in the cooled melted butter, then knead until the almond paste holds together. Don't overknead or it will become greasy. Cover and chill in the refrigerator while making the pastry.

2. To make the pastry, sift the flour and salt into a bowl and make a well in the centre. Melt the butter and add to the well with 100 ml (3$\frac{1}{2}$ fl oz) cold water and the orange flower water. Mix together, using a round-bladed knife, until the dough begins to come together, adding a little more water if necessary. Turn out onto a floured work surface and knead for about 20 minutes until smooth and elastic. Alternatively, knead in a food processor or electric mixer. Leave to rest for 15 minutes.

3. Preheat the oven to 160°C (325°F) Mark 3. Flour a clean work surface well and roll out the pastry as thinly as possible. Move the pastry around and flour the rolling pin to prevent sticking. Using a 7.5-9 cm (3-3$\frac{1}{2}$ inch) fluted cutter, cut out 18 circles of pastry.

4. Divide the almond paste into 18 equal pieces. Roll each piece into a sausage about 6 cm (2$\frac{1}{2}$ inches) long, tapering at the edges. Lay an almond sausage in the middle of each pastry circle, dampen the edges with a little water and fold in half over the paste. Press the edges to seal and bend into a curve. Prick a couple of times with a skewer to prevent them from bursting during baking. Place on a baking sheet.

5. Bake in the oven for 15-20 minutes until very pale golden. Do not overcook or the pastry will be rock hard. Sprinkle with orange flower water whilst still warm and roll in sifted icing sugar to coat generously. Transfer to a wire rack to cool. The crescents are best consumed while still warm, but they will keep in an airtight tin for up to 2 days.

NOTE: If orange flower water is unavailable, for the pastry use the grated rind and juice of 1 small orange instead; sprinkle the cooked crescents with orange juice.

TECHNIQUE

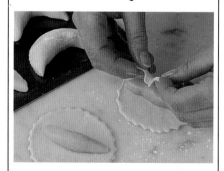

Fold the pastry over the almond paste to enclose, then press the dampened edges together to seal.

GINGERBREAD NATIVITY

This spicy gingerbread stable with its simple figures is easier to make than it looks – especially if you follow the step-by-step guide (on pages 8-9) and use the template outlines provided. If it seems like too much work, try making tree decorations instead. Simply stamp out stars, trees etc, using suitable cutters and make a small hole in the top of each one – to enable a ribbon to be threaded through after baking, for hanging on the tree.

MAKES 1 NATIVITY

350 g (12 oz) plain white flour
5 ml (1 tsp) bicarbonate of soda
30 ml (2 tbsp) ground ginger
15 ml (1 tbsp) ground cinnamon
2.5 ml (½ tsp) ground cloves
125 g (4 oz) butter
175 g (6 oz) soft light brown sugar
60 ml (2 tbsp) golden syrup
1 egg (size 4)
CARAMEL
125 g (4 oz) caster sugar
30 ml (2 tbsp) water
TO DECORATE
twiglets or lean straw matting
demerara and/or other brown sugars, for sprinkling
a little glacé or royal icing
food colourings
edible gold leaf or lustre powder
few toffees or flat sweets

PREPARATION TIME
About 2 hours, plus drying
COOKING TIME
8-10 minutes
FREEZING
Suitable: Uncooked gingerbread dough only

1. Cut out templates for the stable (see pages 8-9). Line two baking sheets with non-stick baking parchment. Preheat the oven to 190°C (375°F) Mark 5.

2. Sift the flour with the bicarbonate of soda and spices into a large bowl. Rub in the butter until the mixture resembles fine breadcrumbs. Stir in the sugar.

3. Warm the syrup very slightly and beat in the egg. Cool slightly, then pour onto the flour mixture. Beat with a wooden spoon to a soft dough. Bring together with your hands and knead until smooth. Cut off one third of the dough, wrap in cling film and reserve.

4. On a lightly floured surface, roll out the other piece of dough to a 5 mm (¼ inch) thickness. Using the stable templates and a sharp knife, cut out each shape. Carefully transfer to the baking sheets, straighten any edges and chill for 15 minutes. Knead the trimmings into the reserved dough, re-wrap and chill to make the figures later.

5. Bake the stable pieces for 8-10 minutes or until golden brown. Leave to cool and harden for 10 minutes on the baking sheet, then transfer to a wire rack to cool completely.

6. To make the caramel, dissolve the sugar in the water in a heavy-based pan over a low heat, then boil to a pale caramel. Immediately dip the base of the pan in cool water to stop further cooking. Use this caramel to join the edges of the stable together and to cement it to a cake board. Join the roof to the stable. Stick twiglets or straw matting to the roof, if liked. Sprinkle sugar(s) in and around the stable.

7. Using the templates (on pages 78-9), cut out the figures and carefully place on the baking sheets. Bake as before, checking after 8 minutes. Cool as before (Use any remaining dough to make biscuits).

8. Decorate the figures with gold leaf or lustre powder, and coloured glacé or royal icing. Allow to dry before assembling around the stable. Use a toffee or sweet and a little icing to cement the base of each figure to the board.

TECHNIQUE

To make the caramel, cook the sugar syrup to a pale golden colour.

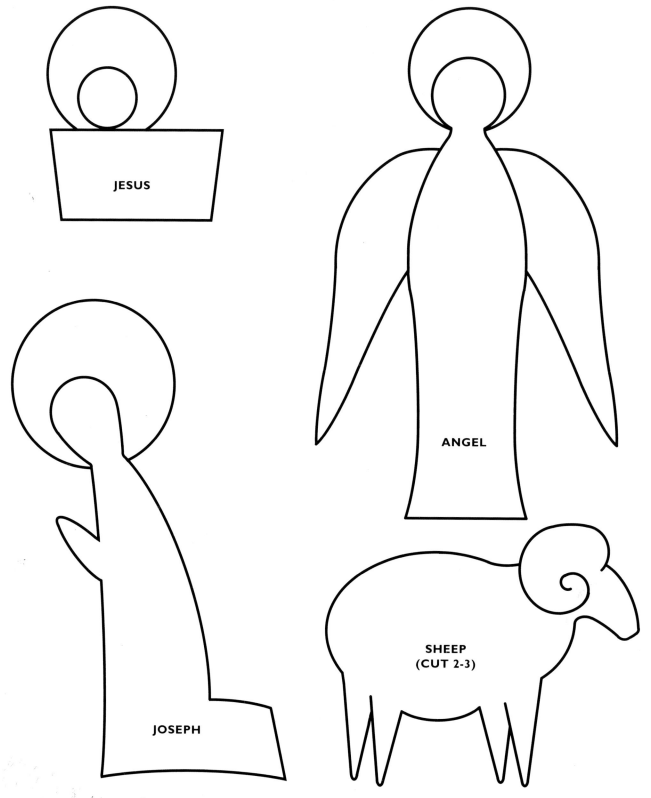

JESUS

ANGEL

JOSEPH

SHEEP
(CUT 2-3)

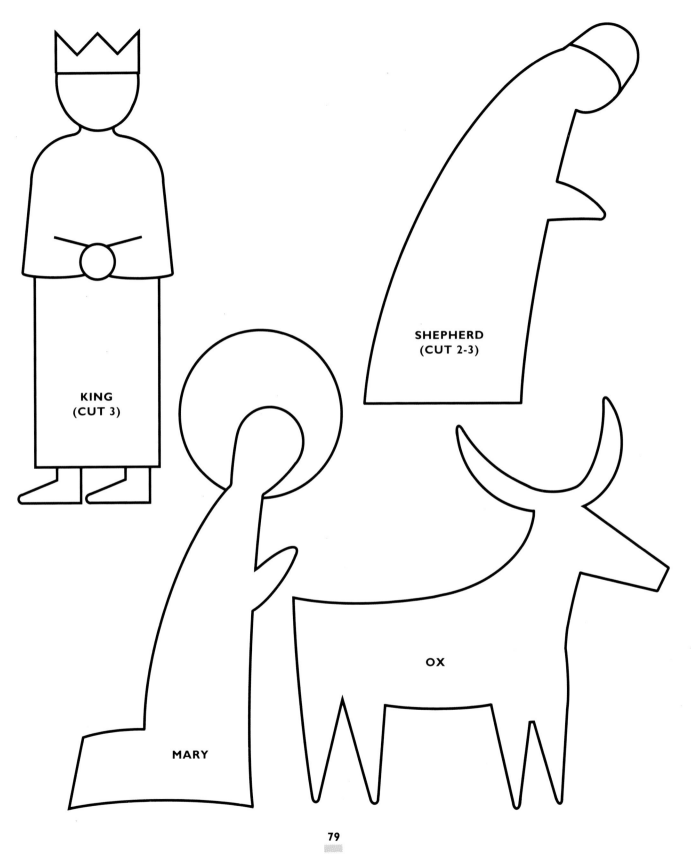

KING
(CUT 3)

SHEPHERD
(CUT 2-3)

MARY

OX

almonds: almond crescents, 74
   almond paste, applying, 5
   raspberry and almond trifle, 52
apricot, pumpkin and almond chutney, 60

bacon, shredded Brussels sprouts with, 38
bananas: mincemeat and banana flan with star fruit, 46
beef, roast rib with chestnut relish, 26
beetroot, cucumber and spring onion salad, 42
Brussels sprouts with bacon, 38

cakes: cinnamon cranberry streussel cake, 68
   luxury Christmas cake, 66
carrot, chestnut and coriander soup, 18
cheese: vegetable ragoût with cheese polenta topping, 34
chestnuts: carrot, chestnut and coriander soup, 18
   chestnut meringue ice, 54
   roast rib of beef with chestnut relish, 26
chicory, clementine and peanut salad, 40
chocolate truffles, 64
Christmas cake, luxury, 66
Christmas cake, decorations, 6-7
Christmas morning muffins, 70

Christmas pudding, 44
chutneys: cranberry and roast shallot, 58
   pumpkin, apricot and almond, 60
cinnamon cranberry streussel cake, 68
clementine, chicory and peanut salad, 40
coconut: lychee and coconut syllabub, 48
cranberries: Christmas morning muffins, 70
   cinnamon cranberry streussel cake, 68
   cranberry and roast shallot chutney, 58
cucumber, beetroot and spring onion salad, 42

dates: pineapple and date salad with kumquats, 50

figs: glazed pork loin with fig stuffing, 28
fish: smoked fish pâté with Melba toast, 16
flans: mincemeat and banana flan with star fruit, 46
fondant icing, applying, 6
French roast pheasant with grapes and nuts, 22

gingerbread nativity, 76, 8-9

ham: braised ham with Madeira mustard sauce, 30
   ham and herb terrine, 14

ice cream: chestnut meringue ice with orange caramel sauce, 54

lychee and coconut syllabub, 48

Madeira mustard sauce, braised ham with, 30
Melba toast, smoked fish pâté with, 16
meringue: chestnut meringue ice with orange caramel sauce, 54
mincemeat and banana flan with star fruit, 46
muffins, Christmas morning, 70

nuts: marinated olives, 12

olives: marinated olives, 12

pastries: almond crescents, 74
pâté, smoked fish, 16
peaches, bottled spiced, 56
pears, bottled spiced, 56
pheasant, French roast, with grapes and nuts, 22
pie, turkey pot, 24
pineapple and date salad with kumquats, 50
polenta: vegetable ragoût with cheese polenta topping, 34
pork: glazed pork loin with fig stuffing, 28
pumpkin, apricot and almond chutney, 60

raspberry and almond trifle, 52

salads: beetroot, cucumber and spring onion, 42
   clementine, chicory and peanut, 40

salmon: baked salmon with easy saffron hollandaise, 32
   pickled salmon on rye, 10
Scots tablet, 62
shallots: cranberry and roast shallot chutney, 58
shortbread, 72
smoked fish pâté with Melba toast, 16
soup: carrot, chestnut and coriander, 18
sweets: Scots tablet, 62
   truffles, 64
syllabub, lychee and coconut, 48

tablet, Scots, 62
terrine, ham and herb, 14
trifle, raspberry and almond, 52
truffles, chocolate, 64
turkey: roast stuffed, 20
   turkey pot pie, 24

vegetables: roasted mixed winter vegetables, 36
   vegetable ragoût with cheese polenta topping, 34

If you would like further information about the **Good Housekeeping Cookery Club**, please write to:
Penny Smith, Ebury Press, Random House, 20 Vauxhall Bridge Road, London SW1V 2SA.
Specialist cake decorating equipment, including gold leaf, food colourings and lustre powders can be obtained by mail order from SQUIRES KITCHEN, Squires House, 3 Waverley Lane, Farnham, Surrey GU9 8BB; Tel 0252- 711749/734309.